ROMANY MAGIC

ROMANY MAGIC

CHARLES BOWNESS

THE AQUARIAN PRESS
Wellingborough, Northamptonshire

First published May 1973
Second Impression September 1974

ISBN 0 85030 106 8

Typeset in Great Britain by
Specialised Offset Services Ltd., Liverpool
and printed by Straker Brothers Ltd., Whitstable, Kent

CONTENTS

CHAPTER ONE

THE DEVELOPMENT OF ROMANY MAGIC

SO LONG AGO now that no one knows when, the Romany people realized and understood the futility of needless possession. They know that permanent possession means an equivalent loss of freedom. They understand that ownership of too much is the real poverty which overtakes those who in yearning always for more lose the greatest possession of all.

To them the greatest treasure of all is freedom. Owning no country, any ground under their feet is land possession enough. The Romany language is universal to Romanies so that they can speak with the same tongue anywhere in the world. Romany music and feeling are likewise international.

Gift of Inner Perception

Amongst a people who have successfully overcome material limitations for centuries, it is not surprising to find that some of them have also instinctively overcome time limitations. The 'deep' Romany has an ability to frequently see things in a simultaneous manner, so that instead of always being confined to past and present, such a person is able to 'see' a whole firmament of past, present, and future, instead of merely observing the individual star.

It is as though rather than hearing only a single instrument, one were able to hear the full symphony of life. Such inner perception is vouchsafed to people of great wisdom through experience, to mystics by dedication, and to natural philosophers as many Romanies are.

Call it second sight, clairvoyance, or what you will, such a faculty is an intangible possession given only to those whose minds are free.

In the same way in which he has acquired freedom to roam

the highways and byways of the world, the 'deep' Romany
has acquired the facility of mental movement. Usually
uncluttered by processes of formal learning, the wisdom of
the Romany is instinctive and therefore natural in origin,
tempered as is all wisdom by environment and experience.

Both magic and science have attracted the attention of
those in search of knowledge, and both have appeared to be
bound up with an attempt at sovereignty over nature and its
laws. In both the succession of natural events has been
assumed to be determined by laws which, if observed and
studied, could lead the observer to calculate and foresee
either events or results. The temptation for such observers
has been to seek apparently boundless possibilities for
expression and activity through an applied knowledge of the
causes of things.

Error and failure in the attempted practice of magic is due
to precisely the same reasons for error and failure in scientific
pursuit; a lack of sufficient understanding of the laws of
nature or its materials.

To the Romany as indeed to most people, magic is an art,
not a science. He does not analyse the philosophy of the
subject, but merely its materials, incantations, applications,
and results. He is not a conscious mystic but a purveyor of a
traditional knowledge, even when the sources of that
knowledge may be obscure.

Two Kinds of Magic

His magic is of two kinds, the magic of similarity or
sympathy, and the magic of contact or contagion. On
occasion these two forms are combined for particular
purposes. His positive magic consists of charms, verbal or
otherwise, to produce results. His negative magic consists of
taboos, to avoid results.

The Romanies brought few material possessions with them
in their migrations from India, but they did bring other
things. Astrology and other methods of divination had long
been practised in the land of their origin and these the
Romanies could transport. Innovations and embellishments
have been added in the course of their travels.

Occult Power

Because of their interminable wanderings and their inherent traditional knowledge, the Romanies have probably done more than any other race to disseminate a belief in fortune-telling, sympathetic and herbal cures, and other matters pertaining to what is popularly known as magic. They have possessed, and pretended to possess, occult power since prehistoric times. By the use of their wits many of them have acquired the art of reading character and thought.

Though frequently allied to deceit, their exercises have often produced genuine ability. Indeed, imposture and deceit alone could not have sustained the Romany system for so many centuries. Within the ramifications of their structure of sorcery lie certain natural truths which they have discovered and utilized. One instance of such discovery in herbal lore may suffice as an example. The Romanies have always known of the heart-sustaining properties of the foxglove. It was many years before the orthodox medical profession began to prescribe digitalis for heart complaints and dropsy.

For a long time now the Romany has served as the humble priest of folk-lore to the poorer classes of people in many parts of the world. There are occasions when the witch-doctor has to produce practical results or be forever discountenanced.

Living Relics

What are often regarded as superstitions are the living relics of beliefs and ways of thought much older than our own, and of beliefs once firmly held but now largely discredited or forgotten. In their time most of them had serious foundation, and the fragmented remains are slender links with a history of forgotten ritualistic faiths. In addition to being interesting in themselves, a study of these fragments can help us to understand thought processes of the past and thus illuminate in part the history of man. To 'touch wood' or throw salt over our shoulders is to acknowledge our pagan origins.

Primitive thought has often anticipated modern scientific theory, and superstition has often been described as the poetry of popular belief. Modern science was born of ancient lore, so that herbalism was the forerunner of medicine, chemistry was preceded by the sorcerer-alchemists, and the knowledge of the solar system held by the astrologers gave rise to astronomy, and so it might fairly be said that magic has paved the way for science.

Real Knowledge

To profess to be able to practise magic of any kind is to invite contempt and ridicule if the attempt is seen to fail many times, unless it is performed before an extremely gullible audience. Two paths are open to one claiming or being assumed to have magical power. Such a claimant can either practise deception, or possess real knowledge.

The deceiver is always in danger of having his shams exposed, whereas the successful claimant merits praise and respect for his real ability. A powerful motive is thus engendered to display a genuine knowledge instead of a false.

Whilst it is easy to condemn those who have deceived the credulous through the ages, it is less generally acknowledged that those who have produced results which have stood the test of time and experience have done incalculable good. This real knowledge by their predecessors has proved to be of inestimable value not only to our modern physicians but to others engaged in every branch of natural science.

Earlier theories may have been crude and some of the hypotheses may now appear absurd, yet through such experimentation we have developed to scientific pursuit of knowledge.

Second Sight

Second sight is the ability to see events before they happen, or of seeing events happening beyond reach of common sight. Only a limited number of people are able to use this faculty, and their power of clarity varies. Some see things clearly, and some dimly. Some see most frequently coming events, others what is happening at a distance. The events seen may be either important or trivial. They may relate to the person who sees them, or to others.

The ability is confined to no particular country or race,

though throughout history certain nations or races have been celebrated for the possession of such powers. Then at some point the power has declined almost to vanishing amongst a particular people, and the ability has apparently transferred to another race for a time.

The ancient civilizations such as those of Egypt, India and China have all been noted for prophecy in their turns, and the Jews were also noted for second sight. More lately it has been the turn of Finns, Icelanders and Scottish islanders as well as others to manifest this ability. The term 'second sight' was originally used in the Scottish Lowlands about 1680 to anglicize the Gaelic word '*taibhsearachd*', which really means 'that which is connected with a vision'. The Norsemen had among their ranks spaemen, persons who were able to foretell events.

Most of us on meeting a friend have remarked, 'I had a feeling I would see you today'. This could be a vestige of the second sight faculty, or merely a buried memory that we were likely to meet at that time.

Extra-sensory perception, usually known as E.S.P., has latterly become respectable as an undeniable fact. It is now generally accepted that human beings possess a 'sixth sense'. The ability to have cognizance without the aid of the ordinary five senses is in most people merely a vestige of a greater power. In a minority of cases this ability is highly developed. In fewer people still, it is subject to conscious control.

To demonstrate the existence of occult phenomena to the public at large is as difficult as trying to describe the perfume of a flower to someone who has never possessed a sense of smell. Equally, certain aspects of science are difficult to explain to those lacking any knowledge of science. It can be readily agreed that not all of nature's laws are understood even in an age of great discoveries.

A Secret Freemasonry

Perhaps no race lends itself to conjecture and theory more than the Romany, a mysterious people who arrived in Europe when events were very rarely accurately recorded. As a race they are a secret freemasonry which makes of them a people as isolated as any savage tribe dwelling in the wilds. Over them hangs a hidden mystery rarely to be comprehended. Centuries of association with other races have failed to obliterate their secret, inner life.

Romanies are educated not with books, but by the hard experience of life. The moors, fields, hills and vales are their estate, the woods and waysides their garden. Their degree of independence is something to be envied; their courage, hardiness and determination something to be admired.

It is a pity that the 'gypsy' has been given such a bad name, for the real gypsy is the Romany whose number has dwindled to a degree where it is more than likely that the average person might never come into contact with him. The trouble lies in the fact that all wagon dwellers are mistakenly regarded as gypsies. Those who have attempted to adopt or imitate the life are not the same as the Romany. They do not have the same deep knowledge of the wild, nor do they follow the same philosophy of life or its laws.

A Wealth of Tradition

In most cases the Romany magician comes of a family in which the art has been practised for many generations. I have no doubt that there are instances which go back to mediaeval times or beyond. This has naturally resulted in the accumulation of a wealth of tradition. The bulk of this tradition is from orally narrated, not written sources and the majority of Romanies, being unlettered, have prodigious memories.

Urania Boswell was renowned for her gift of prophecy. In 1897 she predicted that 'Queen Victoria would see the leaves fall four times before going to her long rest, and that the King who came after her would die long before her own (Urania's) turn came'.

Urania also declared that she would live to see strange things, such as men flying, and travelling in underwater boats. She foretold the coming of radio, stating that people would sit in their own rooms and be able to hear music and voices coming from a thousand miles away. Whilst the *Titanic* was being built, she warned Mr Vanderbilt not to sail in her. He ignored the warning and lost his life after the ill-fated ship struck an iceberg and sank.

Fortune-telling is as prevalent now as ever it was, flourishing in the age of science quite as much as it did in former ages. Artists have often painted Romanies telling fortunes, and the phrase 'the gypsy's warning' has become a cliché.

Some matters pertaining to Romany lore must of necessity remain veiled in obscurity, in part because of certain promises extracted from me, and partly because I have preferred to retail from knowledge rather than succumb to conjecture. I should explain that much of the Romany magic is scrupulously hidden from all save a very few. It has taken me years of picking up scrap by scrap some of the material in this present book. I will however, assure readers that it has been assiduously checked whenever that has proved possible.

CHAPTER TWO

FAMILY LORE

THERE ARE MANY differing views about the Romanies.
They have served as subject matter for romantic novelists and
film-makers. They have been villified as low-bred thieves and
poachers, as worthless vagabonds living idly off the land
cultivated by the more industrious house dweller.

To those who really know them, they are a race of people
who in over five hundred years of wandering through Europe
have retained special characteristics of deep, hidden knowledge. For within the Romany community custom is
curiously stabilized. The true Romany is blessed with a lively
temperament, a fertile imagination, and the retentive
memory of the unlettered.

The Romany does what many of us only dream of doing.
This is why he is beloved of poets, artists and musicians, and
all who seek for romance and mystery in a humdrum world.
Civilization has little power over him because he lives by
traditions which are a secret from the rulers of civilization.

He is looked upon as an outcast of society because he lives
for the present and not the future, and because he prefers his
tents and wagons to the stateliest city dwellings. He has tribal
laws of his own, observances and penalties which are
enforced without fear or favour.

Romanies Inspire Artists

Artists and poets have turned to the race to provide themes
for their work. From Shakespeare to Clare, from Keats to
Borrow, and to painters of the stature of Augustus John,
they have taken from the expressive tenacity of the Romany
people to convey their own fire of creation. Throughout the
centuries the musician has likewise turned to the Romanies
for vital inspiration and borrowed their dances and tunes.

Beethoven and Bartok and Liszt among many others have done this.

Perhaps the greatest exponents of Romany music are to be found in Hungary. There they believe that the violin has a miraculous origin. Their legend tells of a rich girl of great beauty whom the peasants thought bewitched because despite her endowments no man would ask for her in marriage. Passionately in love with a young farmer who hardly noticed her, the girl prayed to Satan for help.

The Devil promised her a magical musical instrument in return for the souls of her family, four brothers and her parents. Agreeing to this diabolical exchange, the girl received the violin on the death of her family, and was enabled to captivate her beloved. After a short period of intense joy the pair were confronted by Satan who demanded their souls too.

The abandoned violin was discovered in a forest by a Romany who learned its secrets and became the preceptor of the Devil's music. His teaching is reflected in the playing of every Romany fiddler since that time, and the satanic instrument continues to arouse the passions.

Melodies, according to such Romanies, can bring storms or sunshine; can cause sickness or bring health. Some hold that a note of music once played is stored in the air to be played again.

Romany Attitude to Music

This Romany attitude to music is Oriental, with a tradition of rhapsodical performance. The musician must string together the songs so that the emotional excitement of the audience grows in intensity as the piece progresses. Such a pattern is exemplified in the Hungarian rhapsody which begins with the slow, sad 'lassu' in which the solo violin improvises and embroiders a tune evoking nostalgic memories, to be followed by a quickening of pace into the rapid melody of the 'friss' which causes the audience to stamp their feet in time to the music. Then, as a grand finale to the rhapsody comes the frenzied, tempestuous 'csardas', sweeping the listeners with its riotous movement.

The object of such music is to produce catharsis, a purification of the emotions, and the primitive style of talented Romany singers, dancers, and musicians provides such magical purification.

So the Romany method of musical performance is closely allied to incantation, and the rhythmic phrase is repeated again and again until it hypnotizes the audience. This applies to the *'alalas'*, the *'gallegadas'* and *'zortzicos'* of Spain, and the *'zambras'* of Morocco, and in fact to all true Romany music.

When we go far back to the beginnings of the history of music we arrive at magic incantation. The prototype of musical art and everything that has sprung from it was the incantation. These incantations were paeans of praise, supplicatory, or mere comfort against the fears of darkness.

Demonstrating the appeal of such original depth in sound, the Russian Tsiganes expressed themselves in Romany choirs under the Tsars, and are celebrated today in the Moscow Gypsy Theatre under the Soviets.

In 1937 an enterprising impresario transported twenty-five Hungarian Romany boys over to England to perform as a violin orchestra. Aged between ten and eighteen, they were a huge success at the London Palladium.

Music has the power to uplift the heart and drive away the devils of sorrow and despair, whether that music proceeds from the totem drums of the Shaman, the Salvation Army, the voices of the Methodist congregation, or priestly incantation.

If there is such a thing as benediction, bringing blessings to groups or to individuals, then it might be argued that there must be exorcism to repel and drive away evil. The Romanies are well versed in such forms of banishment to bring about mysterious results. From the mere war cry calculated to inspire terror in the hearts of an enemy has developed a whole mass of ritual to dispel supernatural agencies. The sound of martial music to inspire confidence, courage and feelings of invulnerability is but another step in such progression.

Incantations

Just as liturgy has established its own method of intonation as being more forceful and more easily committed to memory, so we find that incantations of any kind including exorcism have a more or less metrical form, whether it be a monotonous drone or a sing-song utterance. The most ancient way of memorizing was to repeat aloud the subject matter, and this method was employed until recently in schools for such things as the 'times' tables.

That learning or repeating by rote is used instinctively by children in games accompanied by verbal expression such as skipping verses, is a point to be considered by educationalists.

It is remarkable too that a 'staff-rhyme' is always given by anyone, child or adult, when playing the part of witch, wizard, or fairy godmother in plays or pantomimes containing invocations or spells.

Romany faith in their own secret incantations, practised on their own behalf, is absolute. Since they believe that there are men and women among them possessed of supernatural power inherited or acquired, those so gifted are called in for the purpose of exorcism.

One woman I know, trained from infancy by her mother in medicine and magic, used the following words to dispel disease in children:

'Fire, Fire, burn, burn!
From this child drive away
Disease and devils.
Drive away your smoke.
Give good luck to this child
Make him lucky in the world.
Sticks and twigs and then more sticks
I give to you.
Fire, Fire, burn, burn!'

It may be added that at the ceremony at which I was present, the fire was constantly being fed by the women seated around it, with the exception of the child's mother, who sat with him in her arms. The small boy had recovered from his fever by that evening!

On another occasion the same *chovahonni* or Romany-witch gave a benediction to a new-born boy emerged into life at full moon. The blessing was:

'Full Moon and high sea,
Lucky man you shall be,
Pray to your Moon when she is round,
Good luck for you will then be found.
What you want will come to hand,
On the sea or on the land.'

Taboos

Concerning the matter of childbirth, the Romanies have quite strict taboos. The phenomena of sexual taboo occurs in all stages of culture, even if it is merely restricted to what might or might not be said before women by men, or vice versa. Romany women much prefer to have their babies within the camping site, for to be 'born on the straw' is considered essential to becoming a complete member of the tribe. If it should prove necessary for the confinement to take place in a maternity home, it is extraordinary to what lengths the rest of the family will go in order to ensure that some straw at least is placed under the expectant mother to fulfill the requirements of tradition. Doctors, midwives and nursing staff generally, being humane and understanding people, such requests from anxious Romanies are invariably met.

At childbirth a woman is considered a potential source of contamination in the ceremonial sense, and she is separated from the menfolk by the erection of a birth tent for her own use. Following the birth comes a further period of quarantine, varying with different families from three weeks to three months. During this time only other women may go near the mother.

Protection against Evil

Charms of jet and horn are hung around the neck of the mother to take away possible influence of the evil eye, and protecting both her and the baby. Sprigs of garlic are often placed under the infant to ward off evil spirits.

As soon as a new-born baby has been washed it is deemed lucky to hold the child to the fire, a custom akin to that of the Greek legend of Demeter, Goddess of the Earth, who took a child from its cradle and held it over the fire in order to confer upon it immortality.

The plate, cup and saucer used by the quarantined mother are all broken when she is considered free to return to her normal existence. Crumbs of bread are often scattered around the birth tent as yet another protection from evil.

Iron objects have a significant role in folklore. In terms of superior usage, iron superseded the stone and bronze weapons of paleolithic and neolithic eras, so that it came to be regarded as having magical properties.

Long after iron had passed into general use the belief in these properties persisted, and still persists today. Witches, spirits and other supernatural beings can be rendered powerless against infants if a small piece of iron is placed under the cradle pillow. This was particularly important when it was widely believed that babies were in constant peril from evil sources until they were baptised. Romanies still observe the custom, and even place small pieces of iron around a mother-to-be to ensure a safe delivery.

Baptism is looked upon as a superior form of magic and is performed as soon as possible. After the priest has performed the ceremony, then feasting can take place. Rejoicing is great, because the baptism has provided its own protection for the child during its infancy.

Another reason for celebration is that it is thought that anyone who has been baptised can claim the right to be buried in consecrated ground, in itself some form of protection after death.

Seventh daughters are assumed to be possessed of second sight. The same belief applies to a ninth son. They need not be born of seventh or ninth daughters or sons, but they must be either seventh or ninth in a succession of either sons or daughters, in unbroken line. In other words, a seventh daughter should have six sisters who have preceded her arrival.

Some Romanies will sprinkle a new wagon or a tent with a few drops of blood pricked from the finger of a child. This offering and the belief that the blood of innocent children and virgins gives protection, holds hints of ancient human sacrifice. Long ago, human beings were sometimes walled up alive to ensure the durability of a castle or other great house. This is similar to another ancient practice, that of launching a ship over the body of a woman, thus making a human propitiation to the gods. The modern idea of launching a ship with champagne or wine is a vestige of this old custom of blood sacrifice.

Love Charms

Love and marriage among the Romanies are matters which are surrounded by curious beliefs and practices. If a girl can steal up to a sleeping man and clip off a lock of his hair without awakening him or meeting anyone, she will hold his affections. She must carry the lock of hair on her person afterwards. There is attendant danger in this practice, for if she is seen, the spell will reverse and the man will dislike her instead. A girl can win the love of a married man by persuading him to carry with him a snail shell which she herself has carried for some time. If anyone finds a red string or ribbon, they will find a true and abiding love. Some Romany girls make their intentions plain by giving to the man of their desire an article of clothing which is coloured red. The finding of a key is lucky for lovers if they pick up the key and say aloud the name of the desired. That person will then become their own. If the finders of red stuff or keys should have no particular beloved one, then they should simply wish to be lucky in love.

There is a great deal of lore concerning shoes in Romany love matters. The phrase 'not fit to kiss my shoes' is indicative of the fact that in ancient times shoes were often symbolic of liberty and personal control. Many slaves did not own shoes. The shoes attached to bridal cars are a reflection of this, for the bride has become mistress of a household. Furthermore the shoe and the grains of rice at weddings are significant of luck and fertility. The old woman who lived in a shoe, it may be remembered, had rather too many children!

Many such nursery rhymes do indeed go back to the nursery time of civilization and ancient mythology. 'Blind man's buff', so innocuously played at childrens parties had its origins in the magical ceremony of discovering a husband. This particular witches' game is still used by Eastern European Romanies, the girl being 'caught' is the one who will be married within the year.

Husbands and Lovers

To discover what kind of a husband she will gain, a girl must take the seeds of an apple to a crossroads at Easter time, then mix them with damp, ploughed up earth. She must then place this earth on the road and wait to see who treads upon it first. If it is a man, then her husband will be a young bachelor. But if it is a woman, then the girl's husband will either be elderly or a widower.

To gain revenge upon a faithless lover all that is necessary is for a woman to take a hair from her head and place it in a bird's nest that is in use. This will cause the faithless one's marriage to be unhappy, and he will suffer regret that he did not marry his former sweetheart instead. This spell lasts until the hair decays, which takes a long time.

Should a girl wish to dream of her future husband, it is necessary for her to obtain an apple from a widow on Saint Andrew's Eve. She must not give thanks for receipt of the apple, and should eat half of it before midnight, and the other half after midnight. Her future lover will then be revealed whilst she is asleep.

Another method of winning the heart of a loved one is to take an onion and plant it in a brand new pot while repeating his or her name. Then twice a day, morning and night these words should be said over it:

'As this onion grows,
As this blossom grows,
Let her/his heart be
Always turned to me.'

Yet another way of rendering another's marriage unhappy is to powder the shell of a crab and mix the powder with the food or drink of the faithless lover. This will also ensure that he will endlessly regret his loss of the spellbinder.

A person suffering from unrequited love should crush a

piece of lodestone into a powder and swallow a little of the dust in a drink. They should then say the following words:
'I will make three cheeses
From the milk of three black goats.
One I will offer to the power of the lodestone.
The second I will give to Saint Mary.
And the third I will give to the Devil.'

Love Spells

A girl who wishes to see the face of her husband-to-be can take the front left foot of a rabbit, three quartz chips, a bit of rosemary, a bit of rue, a piece of wheat straw, oat straw, barley straw, and rye straw. She should then add anything which has been dipped in the blood of a pigeon. All these ingredients are then stitched into a small bag which must never be opened up again. She must sleep on this bag on the night of the twenty-first of March, which is the beginning of the new astrological year. The face of her future husband will then appear to her in sleep.

To get the man she loves, a girl can accomplish this if she will drill a hole through a cherry stone each night. The number of stones must equal the number of years of the girl's age. The spell will not work if it is practised during the wane of the moon. Having patiently drilled the required number of cherry stones, they should then be threaded on a string. Next the girl must sleep for fourteen consecutive nights with the stones tied round her left knee. This will make the man she loves aware of her, and she will win his love.

Should an unmarried woman find a stone with a hole through it she should thread her shoelace through it and tie the ends. She should then throw it into a tree. If it catches in the branches and remains hanging, she will be happily married within the year, but if it falls to the ground she will be disappointed in her present affair.

To be certain that no one can take her lover or her husband from her, a woman can make the following spell. All that is required is a nutmeg which she cuts into four equal parts. One part is thrown into water, one into the fire, and one is buried. The last part must be boiled in a little water and the water drunk. This last part of the nutmeg should then be kept always on her person, and she should sleep with it under her pillow each night. No one can then take her lover from her.

If a girl finds the footprint of the man she desires, she can secure his love by digging out the earth within the print and burying it under a willow tree while saying:

'Earth on earth.

My love my own shall be.

Grow like the willow tree

No sadness bring to me.

He the man, I the woman.

This shall be.'

To punish an unfaithful lover, a girl can light a candle at midnight and prick it three times with a needle to this incantation:

'Three times this candle is pricked by me,

And three times your heart shall broken be.'

To show that Romany girls do not have it all their own way, here are three love charms for men. If a man plucks a piece of grass and puts it in his mouth, then turns to East and to West while saying:

'Where the sun rises,

My love will be with me.

Where the sun goes down,

I will be with my love',

he will get his love if the blade of grass is cut into pieces which must then be mixed with food the girl will eat.

Another way for a man to gain his beloved is to take willow twigs which have grown into a 'knot' and secretly place them in her bed. For this to be successful the girl must sleep unaware of the presence of this natural lovers' knot.

If a man can get a shoe worn by his desired, and hang it from his bed after filling it with rue, she will become his.

Hair Magic

If a woman is afraid of losing her husband's love, she should take some of his hair and tie it to a lock of her own. This should be done secretly in full moonlight and on three separate occasions.

The exchange of locks of hair by lovers and the keeping of locks of hair generally, is connected with magic. According to the witchcraft of the world, any individual can be harmed or even killed if the magician can obtain any portion of the person, however small. This applies especially to hair, nail clippings and the like, but by the same token a person can be protected or given good fortune by the magician instead. If a bird should find any of your hair and use it in building its nest, you will suffer from headaches until you take the following cure. During the wane of the moon rub your head with egg yolks, then wash it in running water. An additional safeguard is to mix a few hairs with food given to a white dog to eat.

It may be more than coincidence that egg yolk is regarded by women as being good for the hair, and such treatment is used in hairdressing parlours and advocated in women's magazines.

A salutary warning of the possible rebound of magical applications is illustrated in this popular camp fire tale.

Briefly, a wizard was asked to destroy a young but wicked witch. He tracked her down, and they fell in love. Their predicament was that each had sworn on magic oath to change the other into something harmless. If the vows were not kept they would die. Their marriage effected the change, but the question was, which had thereby defeated the other, the great wizard or the powerful witch?

Such tales are traditional to the Romanies, and may be instructive or merely entertaining. One which gives warning against greed is that which tells of Zuba Lovell who made a pact with the Devil for riches in exchange for her soul. For a while she enjoyed the riches, but eventually her father found her frock and shawl beneath a tree. She was never seen again.

Romany Marriage

Marriage among the Romanies has been a source of popular invention with writers for years. The truth is that most of them are legally married in village churches, and afterwards a celebration is held, and the guests then witness a ceremony peculiar to the group concerned, and which is a remnant of an older, original, and more involved ceremony. The ritual is variable, but at most of the weddings bread is broken and a drop of blood from each partner allowed to fall on it, after which both bride and groom each swallow the piece with the other's blood. At these weddings it is an elderly clan leader who performs the ceremony, asking the couple to vow fidelity to each other, before pricking their thumbs with a thorn. Romany weddings are absolutely binding, and divorce is virtually unknown.

Other ceremonies are sometimes used, including the leaping over a broomstick, though this custom really belongs to the Tinkers, and is not Romany at all. Another marriage rite which has been quite common is that of the mere act of joining hands before witnesses, and the validity of such a marriage has been upheld in an English court.

The broomstick weddings mentioned in the last paragraph are usually to be found in and around Somerset. The broomstick used is a branch of green broom in most cases, although if the broom is in golden flower it is taken as an extra good omen for the fertility of the union. When jumping, if the man's clothing touches the broom, he will be unfaithful. Should the woman touch the broom in leaping, she is considered to be already pregnant or at least not a virgin. This jumping over a broomstick before members of both families concerned is only one of many customs, but sufficient in itself. It is a remnant of an ancient fertility cult, and sometimes a mere besom made of broom is used. The phrase 'living over the brush' to denote a couple not legally married is current among non-Gypsies and is probably taken from this custom.

Romany Wedding Customs

Various Romany wedding customs contain the remains of fecundity rites such as breaking bread or cake over the heads of the pair. These customs are akin to, and no stranger than the throwing of rice and confetti, plus the lucky shoes, horseshoes and other forms of symbolism employed in polite society. Rice at weddings represents a symbol of fertility, yet its earlier meaning was that of a propitiation of evil influences.

At Sulukule in the Gypsy quarter of Istanbul, I met several Romanies who were regularly hired to dance at the weddings of rich people. The presence of the Romanies at these festivities is supposed to bring good fortune and fertility to the marriages.

One belief of Romany girls is that if they hold a lump of sugar in their armpits when going to their wedding it will bring sweetness to the marriage. A bride-to-be should also burn some flowers gathered on Saint John's Eve if possible, to protect herself and her partner from sickness.

At some weddings the officiating clan leader or chief drinks wine from a small earthenware jar. Then the couple drink from it in turn before handing it back. The chief then throws it to the ground to break, and the husband and wife must collect the broken pieces and keep them. They will stay together as long as they have the fragments. If any pieces get lost the marriage is assumed to be null until a second jar has been broken by the chief.

Marriages in Hungary and Rumania are often followed by the onlookers sprinkling the pair with water and rubbing them with weasel skins. This is a general protection against illness and misfortune, but is particularly useful as a protection against death by drowning.

Blood Rite

The most complicated ceremony I have witnessed was one which began by the chief asking both parents if they were willing to let the young couple marry. Having their consent he was then handed a bunch of twigs. Next he addressed the bridegroom with these words: 'In the woods are many trees. Which of them would you have?'

The bridegroom replied: 'The willow, the holly, and the elder.'

These are all woods which are much used by the Romanies for many purposes, and which would therefore be utilized in the future domestic life of the couple. The chief then took from the bundle one twig of each wood named, and threw the rest into the fire. He laid the selected twigs on the ground before the couple and posed the question: 'Do you want to become man and wife?'

Replying, the bridegroom said simply, 'Yes. Make us one.'

Taking a knife the chief then pricked the bridegroom's right wrist and the bride's left. He tied their wrists together with a cord, palm to palm, allowing their blood to mingle, thus signifying lifelong unity.

When tying the cord the chief said over the first knot: 'This so you will be faithful.' Over the second knot he said, 'This for a long and happy life.' Lastly, over the third knot, he said, 'This for many children.'

Then, still tied, the couple jumped over the fire, and then ran into a nearby stream. The symbolism of this act was plainly that of being prepared to 'go through fire and water' for each other.

The bridegroom then fastened his gift of a pair of gold earrings in his wife's ears, and kissed her. The marriage was then complete and the feasting and merriment began. This particular wedding took place on the border of Derbyshire a few years ago.

Identity of Substance

The principle of unification ceremonies such as those containing blood rites or even the simple holding of hands is that of mutual inoculation against those properties in each partner dangerous to the other. Real union can only prosper when it is innocuous on both sides. The ceremony is the visible completion of ideas of contact between two opposites. Each of the two parties gives to the other a part of himself or herself, and each receives from the other a part. The effect is to produce some identity of substance, be it in love charms, locks of hair, pieces of clothing and the like. When such an act of mutual inoculation is done simultaneously before witnesses, it takes on a sacramental character and constitutes marriage.

Such a union has in accordance with the ideas behind it a totally binding force. The act is a materialized expression of desire for union. Having given a part of themselves into each other's keeping, each party thereby has a hold over the other and a responsibility for the well-being of the union. It is a symbolic recapitulation of the whole cycle of the conception of human relations, latent within the whole of human nature.

The fastening of earrings into a woman's ears as mentioned in the last wedding ceremony referred to, is a common Romany custom. Women wear earrings not only because of the gypsy love of flamboyant decoration, and the oriental, traditional practice of carrying one's wealth in the form of ornaments, but because it is considered unlucky for a woman to have a child before having her ears pierced.

Method of Ear Piercing

Ear piercing almost invariably takes place in childhood. I have often seen little girls of six or seven submitting to the operation quite happily, enjoying the sense of occasion, and their own temporary feeling of importance. The method used is for an elderly woman of the clan to rub the child's ear lobes with poppy juice as an efficient anaesthetic. A long needle is held in a flame for a few seconds to disinfect it, then when it has cooled it is thrust through the lobe into a cork held behind the ear. Threaded with knotted cotton, the needle is worked back and forth before being withdrawn, leaving the cotton. The cotton is tied and left in the ear lobe to keep the hole open. This is occasionally worked through the hole, and after the ear has healed the earring is inserted.

There are certain places in the British Isles which are regarded as being particularly fertile spots for the breeding of children. Cumberland, Westmorland, the Vale of Evesham, and the New Forest area are all believed to be places in which children are sure to be conceived. The infertile places in this regard are Surrey, Exmoor, and the Quantock hills. For the true Romany only three things have any real worth; freedom, health, and love. For he says that without freedom there can be no health, and without health, love cannot be enjoyed.

Romany Social Observances

Romanies possess social observances which are peculiar to themselves. Most of these are magical in origin, or connected with taboos. It is extremely bad manners to pass before a Romany who is seated by his fire. The back of the hand should never be shown when passing a cup to another person. A polite visitor would never attempt to poke the fire unless he had known its owner for at least seven years. One should not ask after a missing member of the family until he is brought into conversation by his own relatives. 'Mochardi' is the Romany word for unclean. Dogs and cats are regarded as unclean because they lick themselves all over, but a Romany will drink water from the same vessel that a horse has used, as this animal is not subject to the mochardi taboo.

If an article of crockery should be accidentally broken, it should then be broken a further three times, or such accidents will continue to happen for the rest of the year.

It will be seen that some of these customs are useful in teaching care and thrift, but less apparently useful is the kissing of one's hand to the new moon when it appears. This custom is observed by all witches and believers in witchcraft as an act of homage and greeting to the goddess Diana. It is a custom of great antiquity and is mentioned in the Bible. The relevant passages are in Job 31: 26-28.

When drawing water to be used in magic, it should always be taken with the current in order not to invoke the wrath of the water spirits. After drawing water for any purpose a few drops should always be spilt on the ground as a placatory measure.

It is unlucky to look back when departing, or to turn and wave, and this superstition is not confined to the Romany race, being staunchly upheld by many fishermen in trawler ports like Hull, Grimsby and Aberdeen.

Anything which is known to have been wept over will bring bad luck to a new owner if he insists on taking it despite his knowledge of its history. On the other hand, worn clothing from another is luckier than new clothing if the giver is a good-natured person.

It is unwise to talk to witches on a Friday, as that is the day regarded as a favourite for Sabbats or meetings, and the talker may find himself becoming a forced attender at such a meeting.

If on rising an article of clothing is put on inside out, it should be kept that way until retiring. This is because the action has drawn the attention of pixies, elves, fairies, or whatever name is used to denote witch-familiars. If the clothing is reversed to its proper manner of wearing, the aforesaid imps will be free to act upon the person, and his day will go badly. To be pixilated or pixie-led is bad, but can be overcome by deliberately turning a garment inside out.

To a grumbler a Romany is likely to say, 'Whoever expects to find a horse without fault should best go on foot'. The persistent questioner may be told, 'It is easier for an ass to ask than for a wise man to answer'. Another saying which has gained proverbial status is, 'If a man has no memory, he should see that he has good legs'.

Romany Religion

Religion amongst Romanies is a quaint mixture comprising whatever faith is current in the host country, plus the belief in witchcraft magic, and a reverence for the dead amounting to ancestor worship. Many Romanies also believe in metempsychosis, or rebirth.

The one saint regarded by the Romanies as their own is Saint Sara, the legendary handmaiden to Mary Salome and Mary Jacobe who fled from Palestine after the crucifixion. As they left the shore Sara cried out not to be left behind. Mary Salome cast her cloak on the waves and Sara rode on it to their arms. Their provisions were all lost in a storm, but Sara guided the boat over the sea by the stars and the scent of land far off. Her guidance brought them to the French Camargue. Eventually a shrine was set up in honour of Saint Sara, the black virgin, the only Romany saint. Romanies from all over Europe and even from the Americas make a pilgrimage annually to kiss the wooden image of the Saint. The original, in its faded blue gown, became so worn away by this regular homage, that a new image was set up in 1951.

It is considered unlucky to camp near to a cemetery. To paint any part of a wagon or other vehicle black is also asking for trouble, for a death will occur in the family before the next new moon, though this belief does not extend to the wearing of black clothing.

Romany Graves

Once, long ago, Romanies buried their dead in wayside graves. Some of these are still to be seen. There is one such old grave by a busy main road in East Anglia which is always covered by flowers, both summer and winter. Being an ancestor worshipper, the Romany believes in the propitiation of the dead. The deceased must not be referred to by name, as this might disturb his spirit. Often too, a member of a bereaved family will give up some habit out of respect for its association with the departed. It might be drinking, smoking, or playing the fiddle, or any other form of self-denial in some way reminiscent of the deceased.

Nowadays, burial is in consecrated ground only, in conformity with convention. Before a funeral the mourners, particularly the relatives, keep a fast and drink only water. A few close relatives, sometimes with a privileged and intimate friend of the deceased, keep a constant vigil over the body.

Eventually, dressed in the best clothes and with former favourite possessions such as earrings, necklaces, or driving whips, or pipes, the body is removed for burial.

Funeral Customs

After the funeral the wagon of the late owner is burnt, and every remaining possession destroyed by being broken up and buried. Many old articles are to be found among the Romanies, antique jewellery, crockery, and so on, but these have all been passed on by the owner during his or her lifetime, this being an invariable rule.

Following a death, vigil is kept until after the funeral, at the very least three people being awake at any one time to keep the spirit company so that his ghost will not return.

Sometimes odd possessions are placed upon the grave, such as a favourite teapot or similar article. Libations of ale are poured on graves, especially when the deceased was a chief or highly respected person. This is often done at later intervals too. There is one old grave in Selston in Nottinghamshire which regularly receives this treatment.

There are other graveside customs, such as the dropping of rosemary into them to protect them from evil influences. Rue and starwort are dropped into the graves of elderly people, while the graves of infants receive snowdrops, violets, or primroses. When the deceased was a person who had settled in a house, then horse brasses are dropped into the grave as a token of forgiveness for having abandoned the road life.

The custom of burning a dead person's wagon and destroying or disposing of their possessions is to ensure that the spirit will rest in peace and not be tempted to return to earth.

Some families will form a cross of stones as near as possible to where someone was accidentally killed, and trample it into the earth. Such crosses in the ground are visited at least once a year and re-formed if necessary, weeded, and generally tidied up. This practice seems to have something in common with the Oriental idea of protecting graves from the depredations of wild animals, and the same idea is reflected in the planting of thorn bushes over a grave.

To stumble when following a coffin is regarded as a sign that a person so doing will find his own grave before the end of the year.

Another curious belief is that in spite of whatever compensations there may be for a fortune-teller, such people have a bad death, and those not possessing the gift of prediction are happy to be without it. Such a witch cannot die 'naturally' until she has passed on her mantle of sorcery to someone else. Until this can be done she must linger on, even in illness or agony.

I have heard Romanies express their belief that people living near to the sea cannot die until the tide is out. This same belief was expressed by Charles Dickens in his novel *David Copperfield* when he makes Mr. Peggotty say, 'People can't die, along the coast, except when the tide's pretty nigh out. They can't be born, unless it's pretty nigh in — not properly born till flood.'

A point of view was once put to me by Nat Lee about the burning of the possessions of the dead, which had nothing to do with the fear of returning spirits. He said that the custom promoted a spirit of independence and endeavour amongst his people, and took away by force the greed for possession which bedevilled other communities.

Death of Nat Lee

He said this shortly before he himself died, and since he was my mentor-in-chief on Romany lore, besides being a most highly respected and beloved elder, it might be apposite to honour his memory by describing here his funeral. It was typical of the orthodox Romany.

I sat among the menfolk, red-eyed with fatigue. We had been sitting up through four nights, ever since old Nat had died, at the age of eighty.

The men were angry amid their sorrow. Angry with the curious outsiders who had tried to intrude upon their grief. Only an hour before, a local pressman had been run out of the camp, dodging flying stones and lumps of sun-hardened earth. He was one of several who had negotiated the winding Lincolnshire lanes, looking for pretty 'caravans' and handsome, story-book gypsies.

They had found instead a large gathering of fierce, suspicious families, who resented the interference of the thoughtless gorgios.

The news of Nat's death had spread rapidly among the shires. Ponies were hitched to wagons, cooking pots stowed away in the kettle-boxes at rear axles, and wheels set turning on the roads to south Lincolnshire.

The influence exerted by Nat during his lifetime was considerable, and so his funeral was also a 'meet'. There were territorial divisions to be re-discussed, family and tribal unions to be arranged, money to be distributed, according to 'leis prala', the law of the brothers.

Lying in his oakwood coffin with his favourite possessions, driving whip, pipe, and a colourful *dicklo* knotted about his neck, old Nat was beyond these affairs.

The time for the burial had arrived, and we filed into the tent where the body lay.

Nat's eldest son, Teni, had shared the four-night vigil with

Emperor Smith, his father's oldest friend, sitting in the tent among the candles burning in jam jars.

During this time no one ate any cooked food, and according to custom, the women were segregated from the men.

As we left the tent it came, from the sombre-clothed women grouped by the wagons, a deep soul-stirring cry, Oriental in its bewailing protest at the inevitability of death. Here was no drawing-room handkerchief dabbing, but a mournful unison of profound grief, the ancient cry of forgotten races which gave rise to liturgy and established ritual.

The coffin was brought out and hoisted aboard a 'trolley', with a black mare garlanded with scarlet hedge-berries, between the shafts.

We set off for the cemetery, walking slowly along behind. Teni handed over the mare at the gates, then he and Emperor and two others carried their burden to the waiting grave.

After the clergyman's address, there was a profound silence, until Teni stepped forward and with tears streaming down his cheeks, he raised both hands and pronounced the Romany benediction, *'Te soves misto!'* (May you sleep well).

Then the mourners crowded round the grave, bending over it, some of them squatting on their heels, rocking backwards and forwards in grief. This lasted for a while and then one by one they rose and walked quietly away.

Gradually we all reassembled at the camp. Daiena, Teni's wife, went into her father-in-law's wagon and came out again with crockery and other breakables in a large basket, a hawking *'kipsi'*.

She carefully smashed each item with a stone, then replacing the fragments into the basket, she returned it to the wagon.

Teni got together all the sets of harness which had belonged to Nat, and threw them into the interior. He then poured a couple of gallons of paraffin on the floor of the wagon. Lastly, he lit a bundle of straw and threw it inside.

We all watched in silence as the wagon blazed furiously, an obituary pyre to a dead Romany.

When at last the ashes had sufficiently cooled, Teni picked out the metal parts which had not burnt, and buried them. By the time he came back the Romanies were packing up and leaving. Some were already on the move again, their trains of wagons winding snake-like along the winding lanes.

To return on the morrow would be to find only ashes and silence, and the empty fields.

Romany Christmas

Turning to a happier subject, I know that many writers of fiction have given us more or less lurid accounts of what they have imagined or believed to be Romany customs. Nowhere among the colourful descriptions of 'marriage ceremonies' and other events have I ever read an account of a Romany Christmas.

It is celebrated in a manner all their own. Far from adopting the gorgio custom, the Romanies have their Christmas on January the Sixth, which incidentally is the correct date. The main preparations are made the day before. Turkey is not the dish used, but roast pig. This is slung across an arrangement of six stakes with a central crosspiece, to be roasted whole. Having obtained the largest pig possible, the actual cooking starts at midday and it may well be ten o'clock at night before it is over.

The whole operation requires much joint activity and division of labour. Sufficient firewood has to be collected to cover the holiday period, special cakes are baked, and an adequate supply of provisions obtained. The roasting fire, some six feet in length, has to be constantly replenished, and spells taken at revolving the pig at regular intervals.

The day before, January the fifth, is also the day when friends are invited in for a drink and to view the splendid pig roasting some three feet above the flames of the great fire.

On their Christmas Day the Romanies keep only the company of their own immediate circle, and stay mainly within their wagons. The pig is eaten cold, being carved from the whole animal as required. A lazy day is spent in eating the pork and the spiced cakes, in talking, drinking, and dozing. The main drinks are port wine and other red wines, as well as gin and home-made wines and ginger beer. Nuts, apples, and other fruits are also eaten.

Holly is not used and the only Christmas 'decoration' consists of dead oak leaves tied over the doors of the wagons, the purpose of which remains obscure to me.

The only other ritual observed is the curious one of carving a cross on the back of the neck of the pig before roasting it. This does not seem to have a deep significance other than that of being a symbolic mark of respect to the holy nature of the celebration.

January the seventh, the equivalent of Boxing Day, is spent in dancing and general merry-making.

CHAPTER THREE

LORE CONCERNING ANIMALS, PLANTS AND OBJECTS

UNTIL FAIRLY RECENTLY magic was accepted in the countryside with the same assurance as the passing of the seasons. Corn dollies were made from the last sheaves of corn harvested, to be kept until the next harvest. This survival of an ancient magical ceremony was to ensure the fertility of the soil.

Such popular beliefs, so often expressed without knowledge of their origins, belong to a tradition of magic which is immeasurably old. Most of the folk dances and other lore reflect fertility rites and various forms of magic. Vaguely held notions common to both town and country, such as the bathing of the eyes in the first rain of June, show a persistent folk memory which has been fragmented by changing society and the contempt of the 'educated'.

Divining by means of a lock of hair is an extremely old idea originating in the belief that if one could be obtained from an enemy it was possible to kill him by magical means. A step on from this came the notion that a person's illness could be diagnosed from a lock of hair.

From this again derived the fear of hair coming into the possession of another, and consequently there arose certain defined uses and legends concerning cutting instruments. Students of the Bible will already have recalled the case of Samson.

Scissors and Shears

The Romanies say that scissors and shears should not be used on Wednesdays and Fridays, though why prohibition extends to these particular days I have been unable to discover.

We are all familiar with the imagery of the scythe of Father Time, and people still talk of someone being 'cut'

down in the prime of life. The folklore of this is extensive
and on one Roman coin Juno appeared holding the shears of
death. Many people still observe the custom of giving a small
coin in token payment against their luck being cut when they
have been presented with the gift of a knife or scissors.

I once heard an old Romany explain to a farmer that his
cows would be safe from bewitchment if he would stick an
old pair of scissors or shears in the centre crossbeam of his
cowshed.

Another Romany solemnly assured me that the swallow
came into being because a servant of the Virgin Mary once
stole a pair of scissors from her mistress. She was punished by
being turned into a bird, and hence the tail of the swallow
resembles the stolen article.

Yet another legend about Saint Mary is that of the frog
who met the holy Mother when she was weeping after the
crucifixion. The frog consoled Mary by telling her that she
herself had lost three of her own children. They had been too
small and feeble to hop out of a wheel rut and were run over
by a cart. Hearing this helped the Virgin Mary to accept her
destiny, whereupon she blessed the frog, saying that the
water in which frogs lived would always be pure and good to
drink.

Mary was also supposed to have dried the clothes of the
infant Jesus on a rosemary bush, and this accounts for the
misty blue of its flowers, its being an evergreen, and for its
medicinal properties.

Bird Legends

Romany legend also has it that a robin tried to pluck away
the thorns from the Saviour on the cross, but only succeeded
in tearing its own breast, which ever after was coloured red.

A further story about the robin is that it once visited hell
out of pity for its denizens, taking a soothing drop of water
in its beak. During this journey its breast was scorched and its
descendants forever bear the marks.

Such tales denote the respect the Romanies have for this
bird, and they say that it is colder in winter than other birds,
which is why it will seek houses and wagons in severe weather

in search of food.

No true Romany will ever harm a robin, and will tell you that to do so is to incur a crooked finger. To have a robin tap on the roof or windows of a wagon is considered extremely lucky for the occupants. A frog hopping on the steps of a wagon is also lucky.

The favourite bird of all to the Romanies is the water wagtail, a creature they regard with a sense of kinship. Many Romany families when travelling along the road and seeing the bird, will think of it as a fortunate sign and will camp as near as possible to where they saw the wagtail. They believe too that if a wagtail alights on the road before them and remains there, they will shortly encounter strange Romanies. But if it takes flight on their approach, they will soon encounter kinfolk. It is strictly against Romany law to kill a water wagtail.

Some Romanies will not kill a snail because they say it carries its home on its back, a feature reminiscent of their own travels from India when they carried their tents. Others will kill snails for food.

That summer visitant the swift is on the wing all day long, feeding on insects in the upper air. It is believed that it quickly dies if it is out of the sky for too long. It is also said that it cannot take flight from the ground and must therefore nest only in the eaves of houses. If one is found upon the ground it should be thrown into the air to give it its freedom, and one's dearest wish should then be made, the granting of which will take place within the year.

Romanies in Algeria and Tunisia regard the stork as sacred, and they will not harm it. In spring time they collect its fallen feathers from which they make fans for sale.

Birds of Ill-omen

The peacock is regarded as a bird of ill-omen because it was the only bird which consented to a request from the Devil to guide him into Paradise. One Romany woman pointed out to me a house where peacocks were kept, and assured me that nothing could induce her to visit it. Peacocks, she asserted, were so unlucky that they caused a variety of ill effects including broken limbs, broken hearts, money losses, and infectious diseases.

Other birds of ill-omen are owls, ravens, a crowing hen bantam, which should always be killed, and magpies. An owl heard hooting soon after dawn is calling a soul from a human body. If an owl perches on a tent or a wagon it is bad luck and means that the tent or wagon will be wrecked. The booming of a bittern is another augury of death, and so are seagulls flying very low over a wagon, bringing threat to one of the occupants. Persistent croaking of a raven means an unexpected death. If a bantam cock crows three times at a person, then someone has 'wished a prayer on them' as one Romany put it to me, and to see a rat hopping on three legs means you will see blood spilt before sunset.

Lucky and Unlucky Animals

For bees to enter a wagon or tent is lucky. It is said that the Devil created two animals for his own pleasure. These are the rat and the pig, and he gave them both insatiable appetites and naked tails. Some Romanies include lizards in this latter category and have a superstitious fear of them. Yet whatever may be thought of the pig, this does not detract from its food value, pork being a favourite with the race.

Reference is made in the Bible to ornaments being worn by animals as a protection against being bewitched. One particular reference as to camels is that given in Judges 8. Originally the horse brasses used in England and elsewhere were for the same purpose. In the East today cowrie shells are still hung around the necks of donkeys and other pack animals to ward off evil influences. A Romany belief has it that it is extremely lucky to see a horse standing with its head over a gate. Some qualify the belief further by stating that the occurrence will be even more fortunate if it is a white horse and the gate a five-barred one.

It is also said that most dogs, horses, and other animals can see ghosts, but that only castrated dogs or spaded bitches can hunt them. Included in this curious category is the spaded vixen, though how such a creature is trained to hunt for ghost-seekers is not clear.

Horse Lore

Since bread and grain afford some protection against both ghosts and witches, a Romany will sometimes sew a small piece of bread into a horse's collar to safeguard the animal. Horseshoes hung up for luck should always have the ends uppermost so that the luck does not drain away.

To give to a horse knowledge of ownership and thus prevent it from straying, Romanies will draw with charcoal a ring on the animal's front left hoof, and a cross on its right hoof. This is done by the camp fire, using these words:

'Stay here with me.
You are mine,
Tied by three ropes;
One of God,
One of Devil,
One of Christ.'

A piece of bread sprinkled with salt is then given to the horse. This spell also protects the animal from being stolen or bewitched. Another, more elaborate way of protecting a horse is to dig a small hole in the ground and place in it some grass along with a few hairs from mane and tail. A pattern of the left fore hoof is then dug from the ground and put into the hole. The incantation accompanying the burial of these things is:

'You will never be hungry.
If anyone tries to steal you,
He will die and go into the ground
Like this grass and this hair.'

Yet another charm preventing a horse from being stolen is that of letting three drops of blood from the finger of a child fall upon a piece of bread. The bread is given to the horse to eat. The incantation is:

'I give to you three drops of blood
From the young and innocent.
No one will steal you,
For their blood and flesh would dry up,
Fire would burn up anyone wishing to steal you.'

As mentioned earlier, like all magic involving use of blood, this holds hints of human sacrifice. The belief in the power of blood for magical purposes extends to the old idea that to enable her victim to recover from the effects of her curse, it was necessary for that victim to draw blood from the witch responsible. It was enough to do this by merely scratching with the finger nails. The practice of 'blooding' at fox hunts is to initiate the tyro to a new experience, and may possibly have a pagan connection of taking power from the animal killed, or protecting oneself from its spirit.

The Romanies have the following method for bringing about retribution against a thief and possibly recovering the stolen property. A black hen must be procured, and made to fast on nine consecutive Fridays. The thief will then either return the stolen property or die. It is claimed that black fowl have an affinity with witches and can thus be used in the service of witchcraft. To appease the Devil a black cock can be sacrificed.

To see a frog the first thing in the morning is lucky, but to see a hare tumbling over and over in the road is the sign of a death to come. It is considered unlucky to kill spiders.

Inanimate Objects

With regard to inanimate objects it is regarded as lucky to see a falling star, but unlucky to see a tree falling. In the latter case the hands should be placed over the ears to avoid hearing the screams of the dying tree spirit. Bread or flour should never be burnt, as this induces poverty, and although green is the colour of fertility, green elder boughs should never be burnt for similar reasons, the elder being used for many purposes such as the making of driving whips and wagon seat frames.

To find a broken flower on the road and to pick it up means that news of the sickness of a relative will be received. The Romanies pick young nettles until May Day for cooking and eating. After that time the nettles are no longer tender and have lost their flavour, because the Devil starts collecting them for spinning his shirts. In a somewhat similar manner the Devil spoils blackberries after the First of October by spitting on them!

The Bay tree is a particularly useful tree since it gives

protection from the Devil, evil spirits, destructive beasts and elements, as well as from fire, lightning, and serpents. Rosemary is often carried as a protection against witches. Other such protective herbs are Dill, Vervain, or common wild Verbena. Branches of Rowan or Mountain Ash are a protection, or the red berries of the tree. Many a walking stick or riding whip is made from the Rowan for this reason. To find a stick floating on water means that an enemy will be beaten. The last made peg of a batch of clothes pegs is sometimes considered to be lucky if given away to a friend, and I possess several such *'kushto fiz'*. Carvings on Romany wagons often combine a love of decoration with good luck symbols, horses heads, flowers, grapes, and so on. Frequently these carvings have a family connection with personal symbols of luck in the past. Sundials are unlucky to be seen, presumably because they utilize the power of the sun in a manner not intended.

The most powerful witches have long straight hair which curls up at the ends, and whose eyes turn up at the corners. Green-eyed witches are the most dangerous of all.

A particularly maleficent charm bringing financial ruin and destruction of peace of mind to its victim, is the one in which a lemon is used. This should be green. Thirteen black pins are stuck into the green lemon and it is then secreted in the house or belongings of the enemy. When the lemon has turned black and become hard the evil effect has been produced.

Holy-stones

Stones with holes through them are lucky, being a protection against fire, lightning, hunger, and disease. They should be natural stones, not deliberately drilled, and they can be made more potent if they are exposed to the light of the full moon on three consecutive nights. They then increase the mental and physical powers of the wearer.

When such a holy-stone has been found, these words should be said:

'I have found
This stone on the ground,

I thank the spirit who left it for me,
It will for me lucky be,
And bring me good fortune.'

Holy-stone in this context merely means a stone with a hole through it. The holy-stone used aboard ships was so called because it was only used for scrubbing decks on Sundays. Sailors had their own 'incantation' for this duty, which ran:

'Six days shalt thou labour
And do all that thou art able,
On the seventh thou shalt scrub the decks
And holy-stone the cable!'.

Reverting to the lucky holy-stones, such stones should never be given away because although the receiver will get good luck, the giver will suffer some misfortune.

More will be given concerning the influences of stones, particularly precious and semi-precious stones, in Chapter Five.

CHAPTER FOUR

THE EVIL EYE

AS THE EYES are so obviously a medium of human emotive expression, it is hardly surprising that an evil glance of hatred can be construed as having the power to bewitch. Eyes can express love, fear, pain, anger, and pleasure. They can also express malice.

Whether they can emit a ray or wave-force literally is contentious. What is certain is that the eyes can hold wonderful powers of fascination. The 'beam of light-wave theory' is held by many to be used in bewitching. Protagonists of the theory are apt to make pseudo-scientific comparisons with lightning, radio, telegraphy, radar, television and photography.

Possession of a readily available source of power against enemies has been the desire of perhaps almost everyone at some time or other. If the power could be applied 'naturally' so that no evidence could be held against the wielder of such a power, then so much the better. The evil eye exactly fits such requirements.

It has long been supposed that the evil eyes could be acquired by the wicked, and also that some possessed it unintentionally, in which latter case it has been regarded as an unfortunate affliction. Belief in the evil eye has been world-wide, and may be connected to the fearful closing of the eyes to avoid having to see something of dread. The ostrich myth of burying the head in sand is concomitant with the human feeling of psychical influence being exerted by a look. The loved one's eyes may bewitch in the romantic sense, but the dread of someone upon seeing a corpse is to fear haunting thoughts. In Chapter Three I quoted the Romany woman's fear of the peacock. Being a bird of the devil it has, along with its other propensities, the evil eye marked on its feathers.

Effects of 'Overlooking'

Illness usually follows from being 'overlooked' by the evil eye, and as an illustration of the fact that we still unwittingly use the idea of evil spirits causing sickness we may consider the etymology of the word 'bug'. Many people unable to specify a mysterious illness, are likely to dismiss it as 'some bug that is going around'.

Now the word 'bug' can mean a verminous insect, but also has its base in words like boggart, bogle and bogeyman, all descriptions of ghosts, goblins and other supernatural visitants. 'Boo' or 'boh' is supposed to be the first word uttered by the hobgoblin to frighten a human on meeting. 'Bo' or 'boh' is used in friendly fashion to surprise small children. 'Peep-bo' also expresses that which was hidden. Race memory has by no means eradicated its spectres of humbug, bogeymen, and bugbears.

In Chapter One of Part Two of *The Zincali*, George Borrow relates an astonishing anecdote concerning the death of his servant Francisco, overlooked by the evil gypsy Chaleco. Having been beaten in a fight with Francisco, the gypsy tells him that he will be dead the next day. This horrible prophecy was fulfilled, and had been witnessed by two others besides Borrow.

Romany women are still employed in Turkey to cure those who have been overlooked in this manner, and Turkish Romanies can be identified by the light blue beads they wear against the evil eye, and with which they also decorate their animals. Necklaces of shells, cowries or even simple snail shells are considered to be useful protections against the evil eye too.

Photography and the Evil Eye

Some Romanies will flatly refuse to be photographed, and this is directly concerned with fear of the evil eye. A part of the 'self' may be captured by the camera, and may be used to the detriment of the subject. Not such an irrational belief as it may at first sound, since photos can be used as evidence against one on certain occasions. Other Romanies will consent to be photographed if they are given a shoe lace. This is to ally an ancient superstition with modern invention, because the shoe lace is related to the loosing and binding of ill luck. Long ago shoes were filled with corn or rice and thrown after newly-weds, and in Hebrew times accompanied by the cry of *'Peru urphu'*, (Increase and multiply). The rudiments of this act can be recognized at weddings today.

Homoeopathic magic is the principle of regarding personal properties to be transmissible, and however crude or primitive we might think such ideas to be, yet in terms of language we consciously express the principle when we speak of a 'contaminating influence'. People can speak of their minds being poisoned by something read, seen, felt, or become acquainted with through some evil influence. The idea of sacred bread and wine has certain similarities with this primitive magic of properties.

Dangerous Words

Akin to the evil glance is the evil or dangerous word or words. When the Romany says it is unlucky to speak the personal name of a dead friend or relative, he is not merely prompted by the feelings of grief such recollection can bring. The name of an individual in magical terms contains some essence of his personality. Likewise, to the literate the written word can convey any emotion through associative means. Advertisers are constantly practising this particular form for commercial ends. Through repetition words can lose efficacy, or they can create subliminal suggestion.

The use of sound such as speech or song for incantations, or of music to suit or excite certain moods, is one of the oldest of the 'magical' discoveries of mankind. Some highly clairvoyant priests of Ancient Egypt could establish an occult connection simply by calling on the god *'Ra'*, as definite as our connection with a radio broadcast when we turn on the set.

The Laws of Vibration

Priests throughout the ages have always employed a deliberate and effective use of sound. Every object and every person has a key-note, which means that the sum of their individual vibrations respond to one particular note or chord. Each one of us is intensely affected by sound waves all the time. Everybody knows of the singer who can discover the note which will shatter the wine glass. The story of the fall of the walls of Jericho is often attributed to a knowledge of the laws of vibration. People who like to get the best out of life avoid if possible inharmonious noises and superfluous chatter.

The Romanies are merely following the tradition of the Zen mystics and the Mantra Yogis when they assert that sound alone, if connected to a specific person or object, can produce disturbing results to one side or the other. Many of the doggerel rhymes used by children at play are survivals of old magical incantation, especially counting-out rhymes, these being connected with sortilege or divination by lot. 'Eeny-meeny-miny-mo' and 'Hickory-dickory-dock' and 'Out you must go like a dirty dish cloth turned in-side-out' are very old formulae indeed.

The fear of being either overlooked or ill-wished is akin to that feeling people often get when things seem to be going too well.

Protection Against Evil Eye

Fortunately there are several simple methods by which such evil influence can be avoided. In the case of the evil eye it is sufficient to hold down the middle two fingers with the thumb, leaving the first and last fingers extended. This produces the horned sign used all over the world. Care should be exercised, as this is an ill-wishing sign as well as a protective one. The four fingers enclosed over the thumb is also helpful, and it is curious to see how many people unconsciously adopt this gesture when they are nervous. The thumb-to-nose gesture of the cheeky urchin is a variant of a sign of defiance against the evil eye of the witch, as is the 'victory' sign. Another protective gesture is that of holding the thumb of the right hand in the left hand, and the left thumb in the right hand at the same time. A reference to the evil eye is made in the Bible, Proverbs 23:6.

Small stags' horns tipped with silver and attached round the neck by means of horsehair braided from a black mare's tail will absorb the influences of the evil eye. Fear of the eye is common in Oriental countries, where many Jews, Moors and Romanies wear talismans of paper covered with magical hieroglyphs in a sealed bag around the neck.

I once saw a Romany witch perform a ritual to obviate the effects of the evil eye upon a child. The father of the child feared that she had been overlooked, and took her to the witch at once.

She told him to collect seven bits of coal, seven ears of wheat, and seven cloves of garlic. She then filled a small iron cauldron with running water, emphasizing to me that it must be filled with the current, not against it. The aforementioned ingredients were put into the water and the cauldron placed on the fire. When the water started to boil, she stirred the mixture with a three-pronged twig, while saying:

'Evil eyes, look at me,
Closed then, they soon will be,
With the power of my mind
I will make them quickly blind.
They will burn, they will burn,
Evil eyes, as they turn.'

Students of the occult will realize that the coal symbolizes the blackness to descend upon the evil eyes, and that the wheat and garlic represent the striking of lightning having a blinding effect, as does the three-pronged twig. This trident is the staff of Siva, as well as of Neptune. Garlic is a well known magical ingredient used as a power against poison as well as sorcery, and akin to the Welsh leek in its connections with Druidism. The three-pointed twig was an important part of this particular witch's arcanum, and she kept it hung up in her wagon.

Fear of the evil eye has engendered many charms and incantations to redress its dreaded influence.

CHAPTER FIVE

PROTECTIVE AND HEALING MAGIC

MODERN CIVILIZATION IS supposed to be a rational process, the lives of the sophisticated being lived in accordance with science, reason, philosophy and law. City dwellers are presumed to have precise knowledge instead of blind chance to rule their existence.

Lost in the darkness of a forest at midnight, a man might be forgiven for coming to know, or at any rate to believe, that there are mysterious forces in the universe which can protect or harm him and that it would be foolish to defy them. He would become what we call superstitious.

It has been estimated that well over a thousand million pounds are spent in Britain and America each year on raffles, lucky draws, sweeps, and other forms of betting. Whether on the level of the street corner betting shop or the luxury roulette club, the principle is the same, a belief in good and bad luck.

Superstition is Instinctive

Despite avowed scepticism, it would be difficult to find a scoffer willing to spend a night alone in a 'haunted house'. With all the consummate skill of modern rationalization, the popular arrogance of the 'scientific age', disbelief propounded in well-lit rooms in company, it is yet easy to find weak links. One recent and personal example will suffice. Whilst in the process of writing this book I was visited by a highly intelligent lady possessing remarkable academic qualifications. She enlarged upon her monistic beliefs, professed atheism, declared superstition to be all nonsense and the supernatural to be simply an outcome of primitive hysteria.

About to leave, she knocked over her handbag which she had placed on the floor by her armchair. From it fell a comb, a few coins, and a small image of a black cat. Quickly retrieving the image with the words, 'Oh, I must not lose that', the lady replaced her possessions.

I made no comment on her inconsistency, and she left the house. Had I offered any remarks about her 'lucky black cat' I would have been assured that it had been given to her by her mother, that it was therefore of some sentimental value, and that she carried it merely from habit.

An unfair example of woman's illogicality? Perhaps. Such glib rationalization is a feature in the character of many people today, often partly through the fear of being laughed at for their secret fears and beliefs in this materialistic age. Men are equally as subject to such inconsistencies as that displayed by the friend I have quoted above.

So in spite of civilization and the 'march of progress' there seems to be something in the human temperament unable or unwilling to eradicate beliefs known as superstitious. This particularly applies to the belief that ornaments, charms, and other objects can guard their possessors from real or imaginary evils. The 'dolly-hanger' motorists are a good modern example. However much they like to think that their suspended mascots are merely there for a bit of fun, they feel compelled to keep them. It might be argued that such mascots dangling from front or rear windows or both, constitute a danger rather than any protection. Obscuring vision when driving, however slightly, and having a swinging, often colourful distraction before the eyes, can hardly be best for safety.

Now that real horseshoes are difficult to obtain, enterprising manufacturers of novelties will readily supply plastic imitations. The superstitious in all classes of society carry or possess all kinds of lucky charms, ranging from stones, rabbits' feet, wishbones, piskeys, dogs, elephants, monkeys and what not, to gold ornaments studded with diamonds.

Amulets
The earliest known amulets were carried on the person or worn as a sympathetical magic preservative against sickness. Such talismans and charms have never lost their popularity

and their use was extended to afford protection against all manner of evil forces. Modern versions include such things as copper rings or bracelets against rheumatism, as well as the array of good luck symbols carried by so many, the bit of heather, the lucky coin, the baby's first tooth, and so on. Then there are the 'charm' bracelets which can hold an astonishing variety of miniature objects.

The established religions have not been behind in the matter, having a whole host of sacred objects ranging from the Jewish *mezuroth* to the Christian pectoral cross.

I do not know of any Romanies in Britain who make up special amulets for others. These can still be fairly readily obtained in the Middle and Far East from Oriental gypsies.

There is however a thriving interest amongst British Romanies in finger rings and earrings. The matter of finger rings is fascinating. Originally two kinds were recognized, those conferring power and authority, and those signifying a vow or some form of service. The meanings were gradually elaborated and extended according to the properties possessed by stones and gems which could be worn on the hands. Here are some of them with their meanings.

Occult Meanings of Gems

For health and physical strength amber or garnet are both useful. Anyone wanting intensified intellectual ability should wear jade, onyx, or lapis-lazuli. The latter also makes the wearer cheerful and fortunate. Amethysts prevent headaches, hangovers, and head pains generally as well as inducing peace and calmness. The red agate and the topaz have similar properties. It is also said that the topaz will help to reduce inflammations when touched. Rubies take away idle and foolish thoughts and make one cheerful, they revive the strength and are regarded as lovers' stones. Energy, courage and confidence come to the wearers of the black agate and the carbuncle. Coral and cornelian attract friendship and loyalty. So does the emerald, but it has the added attraction of resisting poisons, will refresh the sight, prevent dizziness and strengthen the memory. Bringers of happiness are chrysolite and jasper. The jasper will also help one to resist fevers. Pearls and diamonds indicate truth and purity, and the diamond prevents madness and disturbances of the mind. The sapphire is the stone most suitable for children as a luck bringer, it enlivens the senses generally, preventing weariness and melancholy. For those who enjoy parties and gaiety, the sardonyx is the stone. Turquoise, beryl, and malachite are all counter charms against witchcraft, and the wearer of the turquoise should be successful. Jacinth improves the mentality, gives good sleep, and protects from pestilence. It is also said to strengthen the heart, and has been powdered and taken internally for this reason.

Gems and Birth Signs
In this question of individual stones personal inclination can be consulted, but a surer guide is the ruling of astrology corresponding to the birth planet.

Thus Arians should use the diamond, a sign of constancy. Taurus people should wear the emerald for luck, and Gemini people the agate. Those influenced by Cancer the Crab will find the ruby a safeguard against danger, and the people of Leo need the sardonyx. For Virgo subjects there is the chrysolite, and for Librans the opal, which is unlucky for others but not for them. Scorpions will be helped by the topaz, while the turquoise is for Sagittarians. For those born under Capricorn the garnet, standing for their qualities of faithfulness, is the stone. The amethyst, a sign of humanity, is for Aquarians. Sea-coloured aquamarines are best for Pisceans.

A Romany told me that in the matter of lucky mascots it was best to receive specific ones as gifts, and said that a little fish of silver was the best for a lover. For regular travellers either a miniature anchor or ship should be given. To those engaged in business deals the figure of a stag was the thing. For anyone of a reckless nature prone to taking gambles in affairs, the symbol of a tiger's claw should be given.

Bedevilment Legends
According to all ancient belief every disease was caused by evil spirits entering the body, and these could only be driven

out by magic. Such beliefs in the bedevilment of man are
difficult to eradicate. The wartime R.A.F. had its 'gremlins'
to be blamed for aircraft upsets and major or minor disasters
generally. The Merchant Navy has its 'Wizard of the North'
legends and its 'man from Liverpool', its unlucky Finns, its
whistling at sea, and its unfortunate sailing dates and a host
of other beliefs to account for mishaps of one sort or
another. There is hardly a job or profession which does not
have its own pet superstitions, from the actor's fear of
Macbeth to the nursing profession's dislike of red and white
flowers in one bouquet.

Herbal Spells

In many of its forms allied to sympathetic magic, herbal lore
has produced many respectable and acceptable cures, such as
the salicin from willow bark being used in cases of rheumatic
fever.

One old Romany remedy for severe headaches is to rub the
head vigorously, then wash it with vinegar and warm water
while repeating this charm:

'Pain in my head,
Go to the Devil your father.
You have hurt my head,
Now go away from me,
Home to the Devil.
Go to the Evil One.
Whoever treads on my shadow,
Let him have the pain.'

The incantation treatment for painful eyes is to make a
wash of saffron mixed with spring water, and during the
application to recite:

'Pain from my eyes
Go into the water,
Go into the saffron,
Go into the earth,
Go to the Earth Devil.
That is your home.'

The same process of transmission is used in this spell for
curing a child of nose bleeding. Some of the blood is covered

with earth and these words are spoken:
'I give blood to you, Earth.
Take it quickly, for it is warm.
Give it to your child,
Take it from me, Earth.'

Should a child bump its head, then the resultant swelling is pressed upon with the blade of a knife and the following is recited three, seven, or nine times, depending on how serious the injury is:
'Become soft, become soft,
And very soon go away.
Go into the earth,
Never be seen again.
I stick you into the earth.'

The knife is then stuck into the ground the necessary three, seven, or nine times.

The carrying of three wild horse-chestnuts on the person is a strong charm against evil, as well as a protection against rheumatism and allied complaints. If three horse-chestnuts are hidden in the bed of a loved one without their knowledge and at full moon, the person will have good health. Three crosses should be 'drawn' on the bed before placing the chestnuts. By 'drawn' is meant simply making the signs with the finger, and the power of the spell is greatly increased if the bed is in a position in which the moonlight falls across it.

For cataract pick the blue flower of the speedwell and boil it in rain water that has fallen in May. Stir the mixture well and after bottling it strain it and drink a glassful cold, morning and night, and wash the eyes with it twice a day.

For arthritis one should cook stinging nettles and eat them, and drink the water in which they have boiled.

To be safe from all kinds of sorcery take a bunch of squilla and tie it to the main door of the house. It will protect all the inhabitants. Squilla is a plant of the lily family, with blue or purple bell-shaped flowers.

To keep witches away for a year at a time, take a twig from a rowan tree on the second of May, then wrap it in red cotton or thread wound round and round it, and keep it in the window until the next second of May when the same process should be repeated.

A dried weasel's liver will preserve its possessor from drowning.

An old treatment for an external tumour is to take a root of vervain and cut it in half. One half is hung round the neck and the other half in the smoke of the fire. As the second half dries up the tumour disappears.

The eggs of owls taken in omelette form are held to cure certain forms of madness and also alcoholism.

I have heard of Romanies giving decoctions of misletoe boiled with rye flour for cases of epilepsy, but I myself would hesitate to experiment in this direction. Obviously, readers should be guided by common sense in these matters and take only qualified advice.

More Romany Spells

Another old Romany spell is that of cutting down a young willow tree on the eve of St George's Day (23rd April) and setting it up with garlands of flowers. Pregnant women then leave one of their garments underneath it all night. If a leaf or leaves have fallen on the garment by next morning, then childbirth will be easy. Old and sick people can also go to the tree that night and spit on it three times, saying, 'You will soon die, but let me live.' This practice has some affinity with the English May Pole rituals.

Some Romanies will take a wooden box and place herbs in it along with the dried carcass of a snake which everyone in the group must have touched. The box is then carried from tent to tent or wagon to wagon, and everyone must spit on the snake. The carrier of the box must be the oldest man. Then the box and the scapegoat snake are thrown into a river. This spell dispels all the illnesses which would have afflicted the tribe during the ensuing year. If anyone should find the box and open it, then he and his will suffer the illnesses. This particular ritual can only be carried out on the night of Easter Sunday.

One old Romany woman once told me how she produced an abortion on an unfortunate young woman by getting her while fasting, to drink a decoction of parsley root boiled in white wine. This procedure was accompanied by a kind of prayer made to the Devil by the Romany. She refused to tell me the words of supplication spoken to Satan. The same witch told me how her grandmother had once helped to lay an earth-bound spirit. While pregnant with her first child she had gone to the haunted spot with a clergyman. With them they had taken a spaded bitch and a bantam cock. She then placed the cock on her wrist and called the name of the spirit. When the spirit appeared, although the two humans could not see it, the bitch began to howl and the cock to crow. The Romany woman then asked the spirit what was troubling it. The clergyman apparently understood its reply, for he gave his blessing and promised to put the matter right. He then sprinkled the spot with holy water, and the matter was satisfactorily settled. My informant would divulge no more than that, but the story was well known to her people, who all swore that it was quite true. One wonders what the Church authorities of the time thought about such Voodoo-like operations, assuming that they knew of them.

Magical Knots

An old English belief still held by Romanies is that the knots made by a witch must never be disentangled. Such complications have been followed by the witch to lead to an indirect ending. The same principle can be applied by the layman, and the true lovers' knot does not allow the evilly-disposed to trace its source. Identically, the intertwined patterns of an Oriental carpet or a Fair Isle jersey can defeat malicious intent, which will become lost in the maze thus presented. Fishermen's jerseys also provide identification by the use of individual design. There used to be, and may still be, women on the islands of Shetland, Lewis and the Isle of Man, who would sell to fishermen 'witches' handkerchieves' with three special knots tied in them. Each knot represented a wind, and could be used by untying one when a certain wind was required.

Planetary Influences

From early astrology emerged the sciences of astronomy,

physics, mathematics, and in part, medicine. Herbal knowledge is almost second nature to many Romanies. As an extension to the ordinary curative power of herbs, I have been emphatically assured by several Romanies who are herbalists that favourable results can be enhanced by the planetary influences at the time of treatment.

To gain the utmost rapid benefit from certain herbs, they should be applied if possible at times when the planets associated with them are active.

The Sun, which it will be recalled, rules Leo, is active upon these herbs: almond, angelica, eyebright, heart trefoil, juniper, rosemary, rue, saffron, and walnut. The Moon, ruling Cancer, influences the herbs adder's tongue, mousear, saxifrage and trefoil.

Caraway, carrots, endives, horehound, lavender, liquorice, oats and parsley are of particular benefit under Mercury, the ruler of Gemini and Virgo.

The best advantage concerning artichokes, beans, elder, figwort, kidney-wort, marshmallow, mint, peppermint, strawberries and wheat, is under Venus, which rules Taurus and Libra.

Mars, the ruling planet of Aries and Scorpio, is influential over aloes, barberry, catmint, hawkweed, garlic, hops, horseradish, leeks and onions, rhubarb and wormwood.

Jupiter is related in the same way to aniseed, asparagus, beetroot, figs, hyssop, liverwort, lungwort and sage. Jupiter rules Sagittarius and Pisces.

Saturn, ruler of Capricorn and Aquarius, holds an affinity with comfrey, heartsease, henbane, shepherd's purse and spleenwort.

Any reader who has an interest in the herbal lore of the Romanies can find more about the subject in my book *The Romany Way to Health* (Thorsons Publishers Limited).

Birth Sign Deficiencies

Those under the astrological sign of Aries should beware of a deficiency of potassium phosphate, because Aries is largely the sign of the brain worker.

Taurus rules the liver and consequently people of this sign

should have a reasonable intake of sulphate of sodium in order to prevent such illnesses as diabetes.

Ruling the nervous system is Gemini, so Gemini subjects require a sufficiency of potassium chloride which forms the protein of fibron in the blood, which is a nerve builder. Deficiency of this substance can lead to asthma, bronchitis and the like.

Cancer the Crab rules the spleen, and its subjects need fluoride of lime to offset depression and the possibility of dropsy.

The heart, the seat of vitality, comes under Leo, and phosphate of magnesia is useful against cramps, palpitations and meningitis.

Virgo is concerned with stomach and the abdominal region and a deficiency of potassium sulphate will heighten the possibility of general decline.

Librans will note that their sign influences kidney action, but carbonate of sodium will help to ward off lumbago and ailments caused by over-acidity.

To obviate proneness to infectious diseases, those under Scorpio require sulphate of lime. This sign governs the lower part of the trunk.

Saggitarians need cell salts of silicea to prevent various forms of inflammation such as rheumatism. This sign also concerns the lower body, in particular the thigh region.

Calcium phosphate is the preventative of digestive diseases for Capricornians, whose bone structure is influenced by their sign.

Jaundice and similar troubles can be offset for Aquarians by sodium chloride. This sign influences the white corpuscles of the blood.

Red corpuscles are the province of Pisces, and poor circulation and feverish ailments can be controlled by phosphate of iron.

It may be of interest to readers to learn how planetary influences affect the body and its chemical composition. In giving these influences of each planet and the chemicals involved, it might be of help in making a fair assessment of individual needs.

The Romany lore is of course concerned with the wild herbs containing these properties, but since not many people are practising herbalists, it will be more convenient to know directly which chemicals are useful.

This is not to suggest that people should rush out and buy a quantity of chemicals and endanger themselves by haphazard experiment, but rather that they may wish to consult a bio-chemist or a good herbalist. Some considerable study is necessary to produce useful results from this particular lore, but here at least is some guide as to the factors involved.

Many people who have read George Borrow's *Lavengro* have speculated on the nature of the poison with which Mrs Herne tried to kill him, as related in Chapter 71 of the book. That Romanies have a long acquaintance with the effects of chemicals is demonstrated by that singular incident. The poison used on that occasion was in fact witherite, or barium carbonate, a composition of carbonic acid and alkali.

CHAPTER SIX

FORTUNE-TELLING

IT IS IMPORTANT in this chapter for readers to clearly understand one point. In predicting the state of personal affairs, if the conclusion reached is that there will be difficulties, this is not to infer that the individual will be crushed under some remorseless evil destiny.

What should be remembered is that there is no period so unfavourable that common sense and energy cannot improve it. Neither is there any period so favourable that a lack of common sense, along with laziness, will not wreck its good possibilities.

It is difficult to find anyone who will admit belief in what the Romany fortune-teller predicts. It is equally difficult to find anyone who believes in newspaper horoscopes. Yet newspaper proprietors are shrewd business men who would not dream of relinquishing the daily or weekly horoscope column, and so evidently many readers refer to them. A fortune-telling booth is always a popular draw in a charity bazaar, even when it is avowedly 'unprofessional'.

People are much more superstitious than they care to say, and belief in luck, good or ill, is a part of daily life.

Romany Sorcery

As far back as it is possible to trace their history the Romanies have professed sorcery, and particularly an ability of foresight. Perhaps the best argument in favour of this profession is the fact that belief in such practices has withstood the passage of centuries and the constant onslaught of progress.

Without a doubt much of the 'fortune-telling' given out on the calling round, the fairground, and the pier, is a simple form of deceit designed to gain fortune for the prophet or prophetess involved. It is also a certainty that the Romanies themselves believe in their own occult arts on a more serious level.

On many occasions Romanies have readily discriminated for me between the spurious fortune-teller and the genuine. Even in the purely commercial forms it is often astonishing how the 'seer' displays, if not second sight, certainly a marked ability to read character.

Character Reading

Anyone, assuming they have sufficient patience and powers of observation, can develop an astounding talent for character reading. Playing on the credulity of gorgia women for centuries has bred a race of Romanies who know exactly when to pause for mysterious, dramatic effect, and to use other effective tricks of locution. A great deal can be told about a person by anyone who is alert and observant, by the expression, gestures, stance, way of speech, and so on.

To a really gifted seer the 'hidden' desires and inclinations come through. The weaknesses and strengths, character and sexual proclivities, as well as the undeveloped potentialities can be 'seen'. A practised seer is not shocked by what he discovers, having the professional detachment of a doctor or psychiatrist. Such a clairvoyant obviously cannot deny to himself the revelations of the less elevated aspects of his client's character. But he will usually withhold his knowledge of them from the client for that person's sake. The gifted seer has the task of deciding what to reveal and what not to reveal. Consequently the client is invariably told only a portion of what might have been expressed.

There are two kinds of fortune-telling, that which is merely a means of extracting money from the credulous, with promises as the only capital investment required from the teller; and the genuine kind of prophecy in which is displayed a true gift. It may be argued that the only way to distinguish between the two is by later results, which might be positive or negative.

Fraudulent Fortune-telling

The fraudulent type of fortune-telling is usually distinguished by its lack of variation as applied to the range of clients. Young women are promised lovers or husbands, invariably handsome, or at least possessing some desirable quality. Wives are promised children and sometimes second husbands. The elderly are told of wealth to come, apparently through a cynical belief that avarice is an undying passion amongst human beings. Any age group or any type can be reassured by promises of wealth or at least of always finding a comfortable living.

In most cases the spurious fortune-telling affords perfect satisfaction. Quite often the client will refuse to divulge what he or she has been told, sometimes because it has been hinted that this would 'break the luck', and also because this is an occasion when mystery brings a feeling of importance.

The fortune-teller has one extremely useful trick, and is efficient in its use. Cunning flattery and knowledge of human nature can be used equally on the duchess or the charlady. Proficient commercial fortune-tellers are classless and can adapt readily to any type of person, having the ability to realize within a few moments what is required from them.

However much of a fraud false fortune-telling may seem to be, at its best it is an exhibition of character reading, sometimes barely short of miraculous. Through long practice extraordinary powers of observation and subconscious reasoning have been developed among fortune-tellers. Some of the commercial soothsayers are not always aware of how their prowess is achieved, and they attribute it to supernatural agency. In fact many of them develop real clairvoyance.

Deductions in Palmistry

Whatever the Romany palmist may tell a client about heart-lines and life-lines and such like, the things also being studied are the features, eyes, expressions, gestures, and so forth. Anyone who has visited a good fortune-teller will remember the penetrating glances directed from time to time at his or her face. The Romany is accustomed to looking into eyes and faces and to making deductions from them. Ultimately the hand is used as a point of concentration, and even the way in which a person positions their hand is to some extent indicative of character, this being specially true of the thumb. Chiromancy from remote periods has been practised in all countries, and to the Romanies could obviously provide a stock-in-trade wherever their wanderings took them. Some of them do indeed possess a glance which many cannot withstand, a fierce, flashing glance.

Another aspect of commercial palmistry was presented to me by an elderly Romany woman in Felixstowe. 'I can tell real fortunes all right,' she said. 'But a lot of silly young girls come to me for advice, and so I give them good advice to help to keep them out of trouble. Really, it is mostly the kind of advice their own mothers would give to them if they would listen. But they listen to me, because they are paying for it!'

Paradoxically, it is usually easier to tell the fortune of a well-educated person, because such a person will think of many interpretations to put on even one word, whereas a simpler person will either take it literally, or at least fasten upon one meaning.

It is curious that though the age of science has succeeded the age of reason, fortune-telling still flourishes. The Romanies are the best exploiters of it, though not all of those self-styled the Original Gypsy Lee have connections with the race.

Other Methods of Divination

In Rumania there are Romanies who tell fortunes by interpreting the fantastic shapes made by throwing molten lead into cold water. Some Gypsy women in Egypt tell fortunes by casting shells before them, a practice which is probably the forerunner of throwing dice. The Tunisian and Algerian Romanies are famed as interpreters of dreams, while the Turks will use coffee dregs and sand among their methods of divination.

Some people of a sceptical turn of mind may feel that a belief in any form of prediction or magic is merely a degrading superstition. Yet it is because there are times when man feels there is mystery within himself, that he also admits to the feeling that in others it may be higher. Who has not wondered at his dreams, his whispering subconscious, a spirit music hardly heard but always felt? And if this stupendous abyss of nature is recognized, even fleetingly, what may not be revealed to others?

Science can cast its lights, but true scientists know that these lights serve to reveal new darkness beyond.

The best known method of fortune-telling by Romanies in Britain is by palmistry. There are several who possess Tarot cards or know the symbols but who only use this particular card method among themselves, and then only rarely.

Romany Hand Reading

Real Romany hand reading is a matter of concentration and clairvoyance. The left hand is used and attention focused mainly on the thumb, its base, and the surrounding area at first. Some see 'pictures' in the hand and some can rub the area of the palm with their own thumb where they 'see' enemies, and utter a curse. The power of the enemies wanes from that moment. The rubbed palm burns and throbs for a long time afterwards.

Sir Isaac Newton once said, 'In default of other proofs, the thumb would convince me of the existence of God.'

Importance of the Thumb

He was considering the fact that the thumb constitutes the great difference between human hands and the feet of the higher animals. The nearest approach to the human thumb is the monkey's, but compared with that of man it is short and almost immobile. Consequently, again by comparison it is reduced almost to being merely a fifth finger or even simply another nail.

In the human thumb lie the indications of will and intellect. Before it can exercise its will, a baby keeps its fingers closed over its thumbs, whereas a reasoning man when exercising will or determination, almost invariably closes his thumb across his fingers. The onset of an epileptic fit is preceded by the hiding of the thumb with the fingers.

Recognition of the thumb as the symbol of the will was shown in the Roman practice of using it at their gladiatorial displays, when its erection or depression indicated their will concerning the defeated. Thumbs up and thumbs down signs are still popular today.

If the outermost phalange of the thumb is short and narrow, it shows a person weak of will, prone to accept ideas and notions from others without much question, with tendencies to personal feelings of doubt and uncertainty, preferring to be guided by others.

Those with entirely small thumbs are much more sentimental than those with proportionate or large ones, and they are given to acting on impulse rather than reflection.

A large thumb usually indicates an independent spirit and a tendency to despotism and power, but it is a power of force rather than of charm. People with a taste for serious study of the occult have large thumbs. Such people can achieve things not essentially in their nature, for example a large-thumbed mechanic may bring himself to write poetry forms.

The small-thumbed may have tendencies to creative pursuits such as writing poetry, but will lack the talent to cultivate them.

The Fingers

When the Romany palmist looks at a hand he can tell quite a lot from the fingers apart from the actual reading of the palm. For example, at the base of each finger where it joins the palm there is a crease or line. When these creases occur level with each other to form a straight line across the palm from edge to edge, it denotes great self-discipline. Yet there is also a lack of flexibility in the nature of such a person, who insists at times on an unimaginative and rigid correctness of behaviour.

When the creases at the roots of the fingers are uneven, forming an irregular pattern across the top of the palm, it indicates a person who is affected by nervous apprehension.

The balance between these two states is shown when the creases form a gentle arch coming to its highest point below the middle finger.

The Thumb

As already mentioned matters concerning will power are mainly associated with the thumbs. The top phalange shows the will and the bottom phalange the capacity for reasoning. If the thumb is long, powers of reasoning and determination are strong. This is the person who can succeed with ambitions, having aims at singular personal achievements. The chief danger to such people however, is that they may hinder themselves through obstinacy.

When the thumb is short outstanding progress is more difficult to achieve. The owner of a short thumb is best in some pursuit in which team work is required. Under good direction he can work well and be happy, and prefers not to have to organize on an executive level.

The lower phalanges of the fingers tell something about appetites for food and physical comfort. Well-fleshed pads adjoining the palms belong to those who love eating. Such chubby lower segments to the fingers in a woman generally indicate a good cook and one who will provide a comfortable home. In a man it shows a hearty appetite and an appreciation of comfort.

If these root segments of the fingers are flat or thin, it means a fastidious eater, sometimes difficult to please, and apt to be critical. It does however, indicate a person who believes in quality.

The Forefinger

A long forefinger is one not set low in the palm, and its top reaches at least halfway above the middle of the upper phalange of the middle finger. A short forefinger often barely reaches the base of the top phalange of the middle finger.

The person with a long forefinger has ability to take the lead if necessary, can assume authority, but the person with a short forefinger should avoid situations which demand responsibilities he cannot handle.

The Middle Finger

When the middle finger is long and straight it shows a good sense of direction and common sense. If extremely long, dominating the other fingers, it shows too much introversion, excessive caution, and a possibly morbid outlook, suspicious and pessimistic.

If the middle finger is short, being not much longer than either the first or third finger whichever is the longer of those two, it betrays some irresponsibility and a lack of understanding in dealing with other people.

The Third Finger

The third finger is indicative of the propensities for taking chances. If it comes almost to the top of the top-most phalange of the middle finger it is the normal average and shows an ordinary healthy sense of optimism. If however the third finger is as long as the middle finger, it shows a dangerous tendency to take risks either physically or otherwise. Such people may well be inveterate gamblers with a passion for some form of betting. Yet if the third finger reaches to some two-thirds of the top phalange of the middle finger, there is an idealized appreciation of beauty. When the third finger does not even reach to mid-point of the top phalange it suggests tendencies to gaudiness, and flashy colour schemes in dress and decor.

The Little Finger

The little finger, if well-shaped and going above the ring of the top phalange of the third finger, reveals self-control, good manners and behaviour, and also often great ability of expression. If it is short and below the top ring of the third finger, it belongs to someone prone to a lack of self possession, giving abruptness or impulsiveness, and ill-considered reactions.

Generally, smooth well-rounded fingers belong to people with some intuition of mind. Their impressions are usually accurate, and they are quick thinking.

Fingers which are 'knotted' denote slow deliberation, careful consideration, or a tendency to over-hesitancy.

The Hand

When the Romany palmist takes the hand to look into it, he can also tell a good deal from its consistency alone. The hand which is hard to the touch belongs to someone tending to energy and powerful action. This is the early riser, who likes to be up and doing. The hard-handed are rarely polished and gentle in manner, though they are often good natured and sensitive, capable of true, ardent love, though incapable of tenderness.

Those with fat, soft hands are usually indolent, with a rather stagnant intellect. The soft-handed always have a well developed ball of flesh on the outer phalanges of the fingers. They have tact and good taste,and affect temperate movement and activity generally, and like their share of sleep.

Perhaps the ideal hand is that which is firm without being hard, supple without being soft. The indications here are of an active mind and a liberal intelligence combining theory with practice.

The hands of many people become harder or at least stiffer and firmer of skin in old age. This shows gradual decrease in powers of imagination, and a lessening of the sense of beauty in the poetic manner. It is a time when such people turn more towards home arrangement, gardening, and similar pursuits. There is less credulity, less inclination to be open to impressions, and sometimes more logic, and even a tendency to become argumentative.

The hand consistency which was described as the ideal is the type which resists this process longest, some never becoming harder, or only very slowly.

Conditions for an Accurate Reading

There are certain simple conditions which should be observed by anyone wishing to have their hands 'read'. They should not be examined immediately after a full meal, for food and drinks excite the bodily activities, affecting the palms with heat so that they appear more red than normal. The same principle applies to strenuous exercise. For the same reason they should not be shown when too hot in summer. If too cold in winter, they can mislead by becoming pale when heat

is extracted. The hand being read should be gently con-
tracted, the muscles relaxed so that it is as flabby as possible.
A good palmist will inspect the left hand first before
comparing it with the right.

Hand Characteristics

Sceptics have said that hand markings are bound to be
affected by the employment of the individual. This is true
only to a point. Frequently there is a greater variety of marks
(not lines) to be found in the hand of the manual worker as
opposed to the clerical worker or the merely idle. But the
effects of doing exactly the same work will not produce the
same *lines* in the hands of two men.

It is a remarkable fact in nature that every individual
amongst the millions of human beings possesses hand
attributes unlike those of anyone else. The variety is infinite.
Yet since the hands are formed for the same purposes, what
does occur are characteristics of type, following on from
which come the highly individualistic indications.

Characteristics of Women's Hands

The characteristics of each type of hand apply to women as
well as to men, although with a few minor modifications. For
instance, the square 'spatulate' type of hand is less pronounced if that of a woman, because of the greater
suppleness and elasticity of the female hand in general,
consequent on the differences existing between the male and
female dispositions.

Man creates, but woman develops. Man has the faculty of
principle, woman the gift of form. Laws are made by men,
morality by women. Not many women have their joints
developed, and so lack the faculty of combination. In terms
of intellectual occupation this generally leads them to
matters requiring tact rather than science, more to activity of
mind than of body, more to imagination than to judgement.

I must emphasize that the following is a generalization,
and individual readings can show exceptions. Broadly
speaking however, women may be divided into two classes;
those with large and those with small thumbs. The first are

more intelligent than sensitive, having an inclination towards study of some kind. The second, more sensitive than intellectual, prefer romance.

Consideration and clear thinking is the gift of the large-thumbed woman, and love to her is more a matter of head than heart, but it is also more free and faithful. Such a woman is never given to coquetry.

Those with a small thumb make love their all in all, and though not so clever as the other type, they are far more fascinating.

The use of the word 'intelligence' is an arbitrary one where it concerns women, for the cares peculiar to womanhood, their natural sympathies, and maternity, all require and enforce a degree of real intelligence.

The collating of the reports and findings of several generations of Romany palmists indicates that the majority of British women have the outer phalanges of the fingers delicately squared. This shows an efficiency in household and family management generally.

Most Oriental women have small thumbs and small slim hands.

The women who are almost fanatical in a single cause or ideal, the political firebrands and reformers, tend to have very pointed fingers.

A woman with hands shaped like the spatula and having a small thumb will have a great fund of affection along with a love of activity and life. She understands horses and other animals. Her ideas are practical and useful.

Her sister with square fingers and small thumb is orderly and punctual in the home. She manages this by example rather than force. Yet if she has a large thumb she is tyrannical and domineering. Strongly marked lines in the palm also indicate this type of virago. Should the hands also incline to hardness, this can mean narrow-mindedness, prudishness and a tendency to make a fuss.

Women possessing little, soft supple hands with marked joints and a pretty colour are vivacious and sharp-witted. Love to them coincides with gaiety, for they enjoy being merry.

If a woman has hands with strong palms, conical fingers, and a small thumb, she is drawn to rhetoric in love which explains, extols, and palliates. She likes brilliant men who can woo with oratory and persuasion, for she prefers this to cold logic and sound sense.

Delicate smooth-pointed fingers with a little thumb show the lazy-minded woman, governed much more by heart than by sense and spirit. Such women are usually too indolent to care much about the realities and duties of life. They may profess enthusiasms, but rarely activate them.

The Romanies say that although the hand types have much the same characteristics among women as among men, it takes much more confidence and tact to read the character of a woman in her hand than is required in reading that of a man.

Second Sight

It is an odd fact that many people will credit ancient prophets and prophecies but do not care to admit that any contemporary human being might possess similar gifts.

Yet the fact of second sight may not be gainsaid. Mention of it has been made in world literature from earliest times. The gift is not confined to any one race of people. All races have instances of it. Fear of it has caused its suppression by the prosaic at certain periods of history, those suspected of it being tortured and killed.

Prophetic vision is frequently found amongst people living close to nature, in desert and mountainous regions. The nomadic Romany is as constantly close to nature as it is possible to be. A well-authenticated case of prophecy was that of Urania Boswell mentioned in Chapter One, who foretold the coming of the aeroplane, the submarine and radio among many other things. These particular prophecies were uttered by Urania in 1897. She also said that she would live to see them come to pass. As always she was correct, for she died in the nineteen-thirties.

Some may perhaps find it puzzling that the phenomenon of astrology persists almost obtrusively in the twentieth-century. Its origins are supposed to be Babylonian, but like much speculation concerning the past, this merely means as far as we can discover. Popular belief in astrology became fashionable in Europe at the end of the seventeenth-century.

The astrology column well known to newspaper readers has become so commonplace that its singularity has been obscured. How odd that such publications are perpetuating the survival of beliefs which are pre-Christian in origin, stretching back certainly to Ancient Babylon, and possibly to an era before that.

Although most people regard such items as a form of popular entertainment, it cannot be denied that they have provoked many to infer vaguely, if no more, that the stars influence human destiny. It would seem that there are few people who do not at least know their own zodiacal sign, and there are others who have some idea of the attributes of such signs.

To the astrologer the 'Sun-sign', though basic to the principle of casting a horoscope, is by no means the only factor required. This Sun-sign is that one of the twelve star constellations through which the Sun was passing at the time of birth. The twelve signs of the Zodiac are traditionally grouped in threes, and each set of three corresponds to one of the four elements, earth, air, fire and water.

The Earth signs are Taurus, Virgo and Capricorn. Those corresponding to Air are Aquarius, Gemini and Libra, while those of Fire are Aries, Leo and Sagittarius. Representing Water are Pisces, Cancer and Scorpio.

Qualities possessed by those of Earth signs are depth, solidity, reliability. Air signs give us human qualities of a truly civilized nature, hard working, yet often regarded as airy-fairy, head-in-the-cloud types. The fire signs give characteristics of a fiery, spirited nature given to impulsive extroversion. People possessing Water signs are inclined to be thinkers and intellectuals.

The above general basis is further qualified by the fact that each sign of the Zodiac is in turn governed by one of the seven planets, these being Saturn, Jupiter, Mars, Venus, Mercury, the Moon, and the Sun, the last two being regarded as planets in astrology. Some astrologers use Uranus,

Neptune, Pluto and Earth as well.

There are many further subdivisions and ramifications which have to be considered in the case of each individual, but the foregoing is an indication of the initial theory. Obviously, since there are many more than twelve kinds of people in the world, very few are 'pure' Zodiac types. Most so-called astrologers of the popular kind deal only with the basic type of reading for mass consumption. This is why you may sometimes find that your newspaper horoscope is somewhat wide of the mark.

There are in Britain Romanies who are practising astrologers, but certain parts of eastern Europe and the Middle and Far East are where Romany astrologers may be found in any numbers.

Divination by Dreams

Oneiromancy, or divination by dreams has been much practised by Romanies. But before describing their methods in this field it is necessary to say that not all dreams are predictive.

We obviously realize that excess of food or drink can result in bodily upsets which can cause a restless night of 'dreams'. In fact most dreams may be regarded as being of physical origin. In order to distinguish between these and the truly prophetic dream, the following process of elimination might be helpful.

Apart from those dreams brought on by stomachic derangement there are also those occasioned by some bodily excitation due to a previous pleasant or unpleasant experience. Another cause is tension owing to brooding over some problem or fear of a future event.

To categorize further, dreams of terror can be due to a slight and temporary disorder of the heart. Similarly, a defect in the lungs can be responsible for a dream of bloodshed. To experience some enormous difficulty in a dream, such as hacking a way through a jungle, or trying to penetrate a wall indicates disorder of the liver. Dreaming of sharp pains, knife stabs in the back and the like, is because of kidney disorder. If a dream contains some element of hypnotic regularity such as the swinging of a pendulum, then there may well be a tendency to anaemia.

This is by no means a complete list of the physical causes of dreams, but it will suffice as a general guide.

How then do we tell if a dream is of the prophetic variety? According to Romany lore such a dream should be devoid of physical cause, experienced while the body is in regular health, and furthermore should be so vivid and well remembered as to seem to us like a warning or invocation. On waking and remembering, its impact should be so great that we find it impossible to shake off the recollection for a considerable time, and who has not experienced forebodings and presentiments at times too strong to be doubted?

Interpreting a Prophetic Dream

Having assured ourselves that a dream really is significant, we come to the question of interpretation. Since many people express an interest in such interpretation and a dream is so personal that it arouses natural curiosity I propose to give a fairly comprehensive list of definitions which can readily be used.

Dreams about Birth, Babies and Infants are good auguries. To dream of a birth means great good fortune, as does any dream about a baby or babies. A baptism signifies that some long held wish is about to be fulfilled, and a cradle or a child's bed also means the hopes will be realized. To dream of dolls, fairies, or of pregnant women means the same.

Marriage dreams which include altars, bells, cake, pleasant music or an actual wedding all indicate relief from trouble and good news. A bouquet means a slight disappointment, and kisses should put you on guard against deception, while horseshoes or processions mean lucky journeys. A veil means betrayal of a secret, and a ring, though it can mean an engagement can also mean the patching up of a quarrel.

To dream of the symbols of death may not seem very pleasant, yet the Romanies aver that not all of these things show ill-fortune. For instance to dream of burial means being close to marriage, a coffin means great happiness in store, whilst death itself indicates a period of good health and well-being. Macabre dreams of gallows and ghosts and hanged persons, of hearses, as well as slaughter-houses all show good health and good fortune coming shortly. Curiously enough, to dream of a tomb is to have a long and happy life ahead. A drowned person means unhappiness followed by great good fortune, while a cemetery does indeed indicate news of a death. To see a hangman is to receive bad news, and a dream vision of hell is to have danger of disputes and quarrels. Murder means that you will witness some kind of crime, and shipwreck means hesitancy and disappointment in one's affairs.

Women as the main subject of a dream are likewise mixed blessings. A queen or other such exalted female means pride before a downfall, although a nun brings peace of mind. A witch spells difficulties ahead and a group of women humiliation. Actresses denote deception, but a fair woman brings happiness. Servant women inflict boredom from the arrival of an unwelcome visitor.

The male sex can be equally unhelpful for sailors, beggars, lawyers, tailors, doctors and thieves bring respectively difficulties, disappointments, financial losses, betrayal, illness and deception. To prove that not all men are bad, the male friend will bring happiness, while the dream postman will, logically enough, bring long-awaited happy news. The policeman provides safety for your actions, as do the workman and the horseman.

To dream about intimate friends of either sex is to gain help from them or to give help to them.

Dreams About Animals
Most of the dreams about the animal world and insect life seem to bear straightforward connections with the creatures involved. For example a herd of animals means material prosperity, while ants denote hard work followed by reward. Bees, as might be expected, provide prosperity, and so does the cow. A lean cow however, means disappointment. Eagles, elephants, foxes, white horses, lions, larks, lambs, peacocks, sheep and bulls all spell good fortune either in terms of finance or personal success. The main harbingers of dis-

appointments are black horses; grey horses mean uncertainty, and brown ones much delay in affairs. Cats and rats spell treachery, particularly from friends, and dogs indicate malicious gossip about you, though a barking dog denotes introduction to a pleasant stranger. To see a bat in a dream is to meet shortly some unsuspected danger, a bear shows disagreement with a friend, and a camel shows future difficulties. Partridges, pheasants, and rabbits denote social gain, pleasant surprises, and new and valuable friendship, in that order.

Dreams are not necessarily confined to imagery of humans or animals of course, and may well be centred around inanimate objects. Of the three hundred objects given to me by Romanies as having precognitive significance, the few following must suffice.

Interpreting Dream Objects
Symbolizing dangers physical or financial, or temporary worries, either to oneself or to someone close, are these dream objects; walls, tunnels or caves, pits, rocks, knives, blood, an evening sky, and oddly enough, beans.

To presage good fortune, any of these objects may appear in a dream; standing trees, wheels, bottles, crowns, bridges, ditches, buttons, bushes, cheese, hay, rainbows, bread, a clear daytime sky, a fire, although a fireplace means the departure of someone close.

For good health, symbols such as cottages, barley, clear water, and apricots are fortunate. Help from friends is indicated by belts, fir trees, ivy, axes, whilst a basket shows a forthcoming welcome invitation.

Quarrels and disloyalties show in broken bottles, cages, clouds, currants, nettles, and muddy water.

There are many other dream subjects and types of dreams such as those of adventure, battle punishments, calamities, and other conditions. According to Romany lore there is an interpretation to every kind of dream apart from those of physical origin, but the subject is so vast that it merits a whole book. Sufficient now to say that although some of the interpretations seem almost self-evident, such as an empty

purse meaning financial gain, there are many which do not
admit of such easy definition. For instance, to dream of an
amputation does not mean that it should be taken literally,
but rather as an indication that slights and injustices are
coming your way.

When considering dream states we should always
remember how strange and unrelated to waking conscious-
ness they seem to be. The dream is a subjective mental
activity in which symbolism replaces the objective control of
the waking mind. In the dream the subjective tries to express
what you would like to do, or have done in reality. It is
limited however to symbols which often appear totally
unrelated to our conscious thoughts, because they are not
normally associated in the rational mind with the purposes
for which they are used in the dream.

Divination by Cards

Although I do not know how to play any card games, I do at
least know enough to be aware that there are fifty-two cards
in a pack and that each card has its number, colour, symbolic
design, or a picture. This is quite enough to enable anyone to
use them for divination, so long as the interpretations are
known.

That card-reading is very ancient may be deduced from the
popular phrases which have long been part of the English
language. Phrases such as 'on the cards', meaning that
something is likely to happen. To put your 'cards on the
table' means to disclose your plans, while a 'house of cards' is
often used for a visionary project which soon collapses.

The first method of cartomancy I was shown was a quite
simple one. Given here is only a brief survey as space does
not permit of dealing with all the possible permutations.
There is enough information however to provide scope for
private experiment.

Hearts Suit

Each card has its own meaning, and to deal with Hearts first
we have Ace equalling happiness and gifts. King represents a
fair man, a rich lover or a man connected with money. The

Queen of Hearts shows a fair woman and a friendly one. Jack of Hearts is a young man, frequently a lover. Ten indicates love or appreciation from someone important in the personal life. Nine means that someone at a distance is thinking of you, and also represents success, Eight that you should beware of jealousy, and can also mean a visit or a present, while Seven shows travel leading to romance or in romantic circumstances, it means in fact the loved one, or the one to whom one will eventually form an attachment. Six is for a special date leading to romance, Five indicates an invitation, while Four denotes a mundane improvement in the home. Three of Hearts gives a sign of advice or other help from a friend, and Two of a visit from an old friend.

Diamonds Suit
Taking Diamonds as the next suit, the Ace means good advice leading to gain, and also letters, usually concerning business. The King of Diamonds represents a strong man physically or mentally and also indicates an older man bringing help or advice, while the Queen can mean the same in a woman, but curiously enough can also mean a harmful woman, and the woman in any case is always a fair one. Jack of Diamonds is a man in uniform, a letter, or help from a stranger. Ten is a journey, or great gain if prompt action is taken. Nine gives a time right for speculative enterprise, Eight means a loan if wanted, or a trip into the country, Seven a gift or your success augmented by someone of influence, and Six means reward through creative work. Five and Four are similar in that the first shows spending for pleasure, and the second a possibility of extravagance. Three indicates that the subject is being undervalued in some way, and Two requires the subject to seek cooperation before spending.

Spades Suit
The Ace of Spades means law cases, but also proposals, though generally it indicates problems ahead. The King of Spades is considered to be symbolic of the lawyer, the solicitor, or someone involved in legal affairs in some way. This is not very flattering to the legal profession since it can

also mean that a trusted man turns out to be false. Queen of
Spades may be a divorced woman, or a woman causing losses
to the subject. Jack of Spades is a young but dominating
man, and he is always dark. Ten is delay and worry, often
through receipt of a letter. Nine is sorrow also often involving
a written message, Eight too is sorrow, bad news, but can also
be a sign that the subject should bide his time. Seven
represents jealousy and anxiety. Six indicates minor mishaps,
Five malicious gossip with possible detriment to the subject's
romance, Four means care should be taken in sifting advice.
Three means avoid quarrels, and Two that no risks should be
taken.

Clubs Suit

There are two possible interpretations for the Ace of Clubs,
either monetary success, or temporary delays in the affairs.
The King of Clubs is a dark man, and also a man giving help
in a time of difficulty. The Queen is also dark, and also
helpful with womanly advice. Jack of Clubs, like the other
three Jacks, is a young man. He is dark and may be a lover, or
a man inviting the subject to travel. Ten means a lot of
money coming, or an important discussion involving the
future. Nine can indicate danger of losses or a theft, yet
curiously enough can also mean marriage with financial
benefit. Eight is a dark young woman, a small amount of
money, or a sign to patiently bear troubles soon arising.
Seven of Clubs can represent a dark child, the taking on of
extra responsibility, or some money to come. Six indicates
boredom with a dull routine, Five means danger through
impulsive action, Four shows a time to concentrate on home
affairs, Three means a change of mind about something, and
Two means a worrying mistake.

You will see from the foregoing that each suit has its own
predominant meaning. This may be summarized as follows.

Hearts are concerned with friendships, love affairs, and
domestic matters.

Diamonds are to do with work or business, and associated
correspondence and travel.

Spades deal with sorrows, treachery, infidelity and other

such difficulties.

Clubs are primarily concerned with money matters.

It may have occurred to the reader that the cards admitting of more than one interpretation are those higher in numerical order, from Seven to Ten and up to Jack, Queen, King, and including the Ace as the highest card. These are regarded as the principal cards by the Romanies, far more important and meaningful than those below Seven.

How to Give a Reading

As a conclusion to this matter of cards I will give some hints concerning these principal cards, but it is now time to explain the easiest method of giving a reading.

The pack should be well shuffled, then the subject should be asked to cut it seven times. The top seven cards, one from each cut, are then laid out to be read, using the basic meanings as given.

A short but typical exercise in fortune-telling by cards would go like this. Suppose that the subject had made his seven cuts, and we had laid out the seven top cards. Now suppose that these seven cards were in order from left to right as follows.

Six of Spades, Queen of Clubs, Ace of Diamonds, Jack of Clubs, Seven of Hearts, Five of Spades and King of Diamonds.

The reading, in brief would be: 'You will meet a few minor difficulties over the next few days, but towards the end of that time you will find that a woman's advice will be helpful and she will give you a new confidence in yourself and help you to shake off your troubles. You will then be able to follow a new course which will lead to a little extra money. You will then get an invitation to take a journey. There is romance ahead and when you meet this, take no notice of gossip or adverse criticism because it could mar or destroy your pleasure. Altogether a fortunate reading because you will benefit from the sound advice of an older man who has your interests at heart'.

Interpretation of the Principal Cards

If you consider this short sample reading you will see that it corresponds to the card meaning given earlier. I previously stated that in conclusion I would give some hints concerning the principal cards. Here they are.

The following juxtapositions may occur when the seven cards selected are laid out. Regarding Aces, if four occur close together, great success is indicated. Three Aces close together also mean a measure of success along with kindness shown to the subject. If two Aces are close together, a marriage is in the offing.

Should there be four Kings close, success is certain. Three or two Kings close show lesser degrees of success.

Four Queens together shows that the subject will suffer through some scandal. Three means harsh words spoken of the subject. Two together means that the subject will attract minor gossip.

When four Jacks are together there will be bitter quarrels. Three gives an indication of at least one quarrel. Two Jacks close together show argument or discussion.

When four Tens are in close proximity a magnificent change will occur in the life of the subject. Three indicate money coming, as do two Tens.

Four Nines together bring much good fortune, three an unexpected stroke of luck, two Nines a measure of success.

Eights signify anxiety, family concerns, and possible anxiety, again in the order of the given formula.

Lastly, four Sevens means beware of more than one enemy. The Seven is of somewhat mixed significance because three of them close show a birth within the family of the subject, while two will mean a new lover appearing on the scene.

Here are a few more prognostications useful to the reader of cards.

Ace of Spades near the Seven of Diamonds suggests annoyance caused by someone. Ace of Spades near the Eight of Spades spells disappointment, while the same Ace near the Nine of Spades means a let-down.

The Ace of Diamonds near to the Nine of Spades indicates

illness, but with Seven of Diamonds it means a quarrel, and with Ten of Diamonds shows news from a distance.

Two indications of short journeys are when the Eight of Diamonds is near to either a Heart or a Club, but if the Seven of Diamonds is near a Club there will be some difficulty over money.

Divination by Dice

Prophecy by the cards is a fascinating matter but space does not permit of dealing with all of the possible permutations. An equally fascinating method of prophecy is that in which dice are used. I had not thought about it much as a Romany practice until I first saw it used at Brigg Horse Fair in Lincolnshire several years ago.

It was a fairly simple procedure. The three ordinary dice were shaken in a small box held in the left hand then tipped out on to a table. On the table was a chalk circle some seven or eight inches in diameter. Interpretations were always made by adding together the number of dots showing uppermost on the dice. There was also a code relating to those dice falling outside the circle, which will be given later.

First, here is the method of interpretation for dice in the circle. Beginning with the maximum possible total of eighteen dots, it was like this. Eighteen dots meant almost immediate good fortune for the subject. Seventeen dots also indicated benefit from some matter shortly to be concluded. Sixteen dots showed a journey terminating in happiness. Fifteen showed trouble coming as a result of some action taken by the subject, and he was told to be cautious. A total of Fourteen dots meant help forthcoming from a friend, while Thirteen was sorrow if the subject were to proceed with some matter already in hand, and he was urged not to go ahead on any account. Twelve was more cheerful as it meant a letter or message bringing a solution to a problem or at least relief of mind. Eleven indicated a parting from a loved one. For a man Ten dots showed that some new approach to a problem would be revealed, but for a woman it meant a birth connected with the subject.

Nine dots indicated a marriage affecting the subject, and

Eight suggested reproach and criticism if the subject persisted in pursuing some matter in mind. If the throw resulted in a total of Seven dots then there would be difficulties, Six showed a loss in affairs, Five meant help from an unexpected quarter, while a total of Four indicated some unpleasantness, probably a quarrel, and Three some surprising developments almost immediately.

With regard to dice rolling out of the circle. One outside meant that regardless of the overall total, there would be some difficulty. Two dice outside the circle brought a quarrel, and if all three dice fell outside the circle then the subject would get his or her wish but the matter would ultimately turn out badly.

The Romany practitioner assured me that the results of such dice consultations always happened within the following nine days, and so the method was only useful for short term prophecy.

Divination by Dominoes

The same man showed me how to read fortunes with the aid of dominoes. Two methods were used, the first for events which should follow at once, and the second method to give a general, wider indication of affairs in life. To begin with all the dominoes were shuffled around the table, and then the subject or client drew one out with his left hand. The practitioner interpreted in the following manner.

Double-Six, money coming. Six-Five showed a party or attendance at a function. Six-Four, legal trouble. Six-Three travel. Six-Two, gifts or new purchases. Six-One, help from a friend. Six-Blank, care should be taken.

A Double-Five meant removal to another house or district. Five-Four gave good fortune through speculation. Five-Three showed a visitor, and Five-Two a party celebration. Five-One meant a romance, but Five-Blank was sorrow, though not necessarily in the subject's home.

When a Double-Four is drawn there will be jollity, though Four-Three brings home troubles. Four-Two suggests loss through theft. Four-One trouble over debt, and Four-Blank an annoyance through a communication such as a letter or a bill.

Double-Three is a marriage symbol. Three-Two is a gamble and a loss thereby, Three-One is a surprise and Three-Blank a surprise with a child involved.

The Double-Two signifies jealousy. Two-One signifies need. Two-Blank other difficulties. Double-One a discovery. One-Blank news, and Double-Blank some unexpected trouble.

A Second Method

Now to come to the second method of fortune-telling by dominoes. The subject selects twelve dominoes with the left hand, turning them face upwards and placing them in a row, left to right. As each domino is placed it should be noticed if it is the right way up or reversed. 'Reversed' means when the smallest number of spots on the domino are furthest away from the subject, as for example if Six-Three was turned up, the Three half of the domino being at the top and the Six spots being nearest to the subject. Obviously, this cannot apply to the Double dominoes. If a 'reverse' occurs it has the effect of halving the good effects in the reading.

It is from the total number of spots on each domino that the answers are given, as below.

Twelve spots (Double-Six), good fortune. Eleven spots (Six-Five), a parting. Ten spots (Six-Four or Double-Five), a change coming with happy results. Nine spots (Six-Three or Five-Four), prospects good. Eight spots (Six-Two, Five-Three or Double-Four), great difficulties ahead. Seven spots (Six-One, Five-Two or Four-Three), difficulties again, with gossip. Six spots (Six-Blank, Five-One or Four-Two or Double-Three), trouble involving losses.

Five spots (Five-Blank, Four-One, Three-Two), the subject's life will be affected by relationships. Four spots (Four-Blank, Three-One or Double-Two), an unpleasant experience ahead. Three spots (Three-Blank, Two-One), surprises in store. Two spots (Two-Blank or Double-One), some difficulty but ending well. One spot only (the One-Blank), means hardships and difficulty. The Double-Blank signifies much misfortune.

The results of this second method of reading take place

within a month, with the exception of the reading for the
first domino selected, as this can take place at an almost
indefinite period of time.

Divination by Tea Leaves

Reading tea leaves is an old-established Romany practice, and
of course is by no means confined to the dark race. Here is
the Romany method of determining fate from tea cups, along
with their interpretations.

The traditional ritual to be observed is for the person to
hold the cup in the left hand, drink all but about a thimbleful
of the tea, then swirl the cup around three times before
inverting it on to the saucer. After counting to seven the cup
is then handed to the reader.

The reader then turns the cup the right way up with the
handle towards the subject and the reading begins from the
symbolism of the shape the tea leaves have taken.

Happiness and prosperity are indicated by the Acorn, a
Duck, an Egg, Lightning, a Sunshade or Umbrella, an Urn, a
Waterfall, while a Castle means marriage with good monetary
prospects, and a Wheel means a legacy, and a Moon means
love and riches.

Quarrels, jealousy, and disputes are shown by a Snake, a
Butterfly, a Cat, Clouds, a Cross, a Dagger, a Goose, a Knife,
a Lion, a figure Two, a Parrot, Scales, a Spade, a Sword, a
Woman, an X, a Yoke, a Wasp, a Finger, and a Nail.

An Anchor is a good sign. Near to the rim of the cup it
means romance involving a journey, in the middle of the cup
it means a journey involving money. An Arch and a Circle
both show marriage either involving the subject or someone
in his or her group. A Square indicates there will be no
marriage in the immediate future. Lucky love affairs are
promised by a Feather, a Fish, a Heart and a Ring.

Changes in life generally are predicted by an Ace, a Gate
(leading to happiness), a Hat, a Key, Lines, a figure Eight, a
Pipe, a Purse, a Spider, and a Steeple.

The Steeple shows change through promotion, and other
success, and general good luck signs are a Bee, a Bell, a
Bouquet, a Clock, a Cup, a Crown, an Elephant, an Eye, a

Fan, a bunch of Fruit, a Harp, a Hive with Bees, a Horseshoe, a Jug, a Ladder, a Lamp, a Necklace, figures Three, Four, Seven and Nine, a Pig, a Spoon, a Star, a Swan, a Tree, a Triangle, a Cart or Wagon, and a Window, which means happiness centred around the home.

A Basket means a new arrival in the family, while friendship is shown by a Candle, a Dog, an Ivy leaf, and a Table.

Danger signals of difficulties ahead are given if these symbols appear. An Axe, a Fork, a Glove or Hand, a Gun, a Hammer, a Question Mark, a Loop or Noose, a Mountain, a Mouse, an Owl, a Rabbit, a Tower, or a Volcano. The Gallows means good fortune and prosperity, but at the same time a warning not to be hasty or impulsive. Letters of the alphabet are the beginnings of surnames of people relevant to the affairs of the subject.

Tea cup reading is one of the simplest forms of fortune-telling and any shape of cup can be used. Those with inside patterns should be avoided as the pattern may obscure the reading.

Although science has found, or may claim to have found, explanations for many of nature's mysteries, there are matters which still defy logical explanation.

Water-divining

Water-divining or dowsing as it is often called, is one such matter. Visitors to my home almost invariably ask me about a hazel-twig divining rod hanging on a wall. The query is, does water-divining work?

It certainly does, and so much so that local authorities in Britain have successfully employed dowsers for municipal purposes. Authorities in Australia and elsewhere have also sought their services.

The origin of water-divining is lost in antiquity, and some commentators believe that the incident described in the Old Testament, Numbers: 20, is an example of it.

It was an old Romany who gave me the 'rod of Moses' now in my possession, and he had used it efficiently over many years. This is not to suggest that dowsing is peculiar to the

Gypsy race, but it is one of those gifts which Romanies frequently possess, although there is little call for them to practise it much today. Before the war they were often asked to trace sources of underground streams causing flooding or waterlogging of agricultural land.

Their usual method was to walk diagonally from corner to corner of the field, then to gradually break up the area by covering it in sections, rather like tracing the pattern of the Union Jack. In this way the most powerful agitations of the divining rod are eventually tracked down to a particular spot, the source of the water. This process of elimination is a most valuable exercise to the farmer or landowner, because he can then ascertain how best the ground can be drained.

The instrument generally employed by the Romanies is the simple forked hazel-twig, formed as near to the shape of the capital letter 'Y' as may be obtained. This is considered best for the divining of water as well as of silver objects. For the tracing of copper, a twig of ash is preferred. Pitch pine is regarded as best for tin, lead, and iron.

Another Romany friend used a rod of whalebone which he acquired many years ago in the old whaling port of Whitby. He told me he believed that about one person in twelve could develop the potential gift of water-divining.

A person may not necessarily believe that amber beads are a protection against witchcraft as well as being a preventative against asthma and dropsy, but in view of the material in the chapters of this book it might be well to restrain dogmatism until a vast knowledge has been gained of telepathy, hypnotism, and occult matters generally.

It does not follow that we should place reliance on all fortune-telling. At the same time we cannot deny that in implied powers of clairvoyance there are sometimes fundamental mysteries which we do not understand.

GLOSSARY OF ROMANY WORDS

ROMANY	ENGLISH
Chovahonni.	Witch.
Dicklo.	Properly 'cloth' but used to denote the neckerchief worn by Romanies.
Gorgia.	A non-Gypsy female.
Gorgio.	A non-Gypsy male.
Gorgios.	The plural for non-Gypsies.
Kipsi.	Basket. Hawking-basket, usually of white willow.
Kushto-fiz.	This is a compound word for a lucky clothes-peg. Kushto means good or lucky, *fiz* being an Anglo-Romany corruption of the word *'fuz'*, meaning willow stem.
Lavengro.	This word, used by Borrow as the title of one of his books, means word-master, the name given to Borrow by the Romanies.
Leis-prala.	The law of the brothers.
Mochardi.	Dirty, unclean.
Te soves misto.	As stated in text, 'May thou sleep well'.
Zincali.	A word used in Spain for the Romany people, and usually truncated to 'Calo'.

BIBLICAL REFERENCES IN ORDER
OF QUOTATION

1. **Job**: 'If I beheld the sun when it shined, or the moon walking in brightness; And my heart hath been secretly enticed, or my mouth hath kissed my hand; This also were an iniquity to be punished by the judge: for I should have denied the God that is above.'

2. **Judges**: 'And she caused him to shave off the seven locks of his head; and she began to afflict him, and his strength went from him.'

3. **Judges**: 'And the weight of the golden earrings that he requested was a thousand and seven hundred shekels of gold; beside ornaments, and collars, and purple raiment that was on the kings of Midian, and beside the chains that were about their camels' necks.'

4. **Proverbs**: 'Eat thou not the bread of him that hath an evil eye, neither desire thou his dainty meats.'

5. **Numbers**: 'And Moses lifted up his hand, and with his rod he smote the rock twice; and the water came out abundantly, and the congregation drank, and their beasts also.'

INDEX